*When everything
goes wrong...there is*

Hope
For The
Hard Times

by
Larry R. Smith

Library of Congress Catalog Card Number 94-075554
International Standard Book Number 0-88243-349-0
Printed in the United States of America

CONTENTS

Hope may be much more important than we have given it credit for. I'm not talking about just any hope, but rather about a strong biblical bedrock kind of hope that can keep us through any of the problems of life. As together we will see, hope can lead us to a firm faith and lasting love. It is a beginning point in being truly strong through all the struggles of life.

This is a very personal book. Many of the illustrations are personal lessons I've learned through trials. I am still learning that problems cannot destroy us unless we let them. I am not approaching this from an ultra-optimistic viewpoint, but neither do I believe I am a pessimist. I view myself as a Christian realist. I realize bad things do happen to good people, but I also know hope holds on to the real and the important things of life. With God's help, we can make it through anything; that's the kind of hope I want to always have. I believe we can have hope even for the really hard times.

This book examines the kind of hope that can get us through the toughest of life's struggles. It looks at some of the hard things we face in life, and how hope helps us in those times. It also leads us to see other aspects of hope that may help us build an ongoing, enduring, life-long hope.

Hard times come. When they come, or if you are in such times now, don't worry, don't quit. There is hope even in the hard times!

It was April 29, 1991. The U.S. Embassy called with a warden message saying that they expected a cyclone to hit the southeastern part of Bangladesh at a point somewhere between Chittagong, the second largest city of Bangladesh, and the sandy Cox's Bazaar area in the far south, near the Burma border. The message said that the cyclone was expected to come inland around seven that evening. They advised all people to stay inside.

I warned the staff members about the possible severity of the coming storm. We had been hearing about the "depression in the bay" and the possible cyclone, but such depressions are common in the Bay of Bengal.

As evening wore on, I anticipated high winds and driving rain that also are common in Bangladesh. I had been through more than my share of disasters in the dozen years our family had been in the country. Even one exposure to disaster is more than anyone should care to experience. Only a few years before, another storm and tidal wave had killed twenty thousand people or more.

We woke the next morning to no significant weather in Dhaka. Business went on as usual. We had breakfast, the kids went to school, and Sharon and I went to the church center. Nothing unusual. Through the busyness of the morning, I heard little of the storm and read nothing until lunchtime when I casually glanced through the paper. The first reports in the paper that day said that maybe a thousand or so were dead.

It is easy to become calloused to other people's problems, especially if the people aren't known or near. Unfortunately, when we heard in other storm reports of thousands who had died, a thousand didn't seem nearly as tragic as what we expected due to the advance warnings.

The intensity of the cyclone was greater than previous storms, with winds of 145 to 160 miles per hour. The high winds created a tidal wave well over twenty-five feet high that literally swept across some of the outlying islands as well as surging inland on the coasts of the mainland. Untold numbers were washed out to sea never to be seen or heard from again.

Kutubdia is one of the larger of those outlying islands that lies twenty to thirty miles south of Chittagong. It was one of the hardest hit areas of the storm. Of the over 120,000 inhabitants, more than 40,000 were reported killed. Most of the homes, crops, livestock, and personal possessions of the islanders were destroyed. The water sources of the island were spoiled by the saltwater from the sea or by dead bodies that were still being found at the bottom of ponds weeks after the storm. Health conditions were deplorable. A month after the storm, hundreds of people still had untreated wounds they had received from the flying or floating debris. Disease was increasing by the day. Due to the enormity of the disaster and the great difficulty of getting to such outlying areas, providing relief was almost impossible for many days after the actual storm. Survivors were left in desperate conditions.

Several from the church were able to go down to areas near Chittagong just days after the storm had hit. The stench of death permeated the several square miles that we visited in the Patenga area, which is literally at the end of the runway of the Chittagong airport. Many dead animals as well as human corpses were still unburied because so many were either killed in those areas or washed ashore at the nearby coast of the Bay of Bengal.

We were able to mount a small, but effective, relief program to feed many of those who had had no food for days. Later a medical team was able to come in, and we were able to bring the first relief medical teams to the island of Kutubdia. In four days we saw over two thousand patients.

To make matters worse, just a few days later, on May 7, tornadoes touched down north of Dhaka, killing nearly fifty people, injuring over a thousand, and destroying twelve villages. This was followed two days later by a storm that killed twenty-seven, only to be followed by another storm that killed another twenty-two.

Ten million were affected by the cyclone, but on top of that, a small earthquake then unsettled one of the riverways. The earthquake and the overabundance of rain combined to cause flooding in the north, destroying even more homes and lives where another three million people were affected.

This all happened in one of the world's poorest countries where the per capita income was at that time only about $130 per person per year. I can't think of a situation more hopeless than that of the people we saw in Kutubdia or the millions of others who were caught in the floods or the aftermath of the tornadoes. Even if they built back most would have nothing because they had almost nothing to start with.

One of the interesting things to me is that in the face of such devastation, people were not throwing themselves off of buildings or slitting their wrists or taking overdoses of drugs to end it all like those we have heard of in pressing times such as the great stock market downturns. Instead, even with the stench of dead bodies all around, a vivid picture in my mind was of people picking up woven bamboo sections, once a part of the walls of their simple mud-and-cow-dung-floored bamboo homes, to construct a simple shelter to protect them from the rains that continued on and off for days.

They did not have much to look forward to—no promises of help from anyone; certainly there were no homeowner's insurance policies on their bamboo huts. Maybe some relief would come, maybe not. Many had no food, and even the meager belongings that kept them at a survival level were gone. Yet, they were rebuilding. An element of hope in what I was seeing made me question why others in less stressful situations give up hope.

Hope is not necessarily triumphant as we can sometimes picture it to be. It is not always light and airy, uplifting us and our emotions to some sort of ecstasy above the hurt and dirt. Hope is more effective in the trenches of possible defeat, giving us at least one possible small step to go forward, one more chance, one more daybreak. A real, solid hope helps us hold on during the hard times.

CHAPTER ONE

An Anchor
for the Soul

Real hope is not something easily done. Go ahead and try to if you can; *do* a hope. Can't, can you? It is not an activity to be turned on or off, is it? Hope is a gift offered to us. Real, solid hope then is to be grasped and held on to, especially in the hard times.

A strong hope that is based on a firm position in Christ may not necessarily change your circumstances. Hope may not change the way people view you or deal with you. (I believe that most people find it is easier to deal with a hopeful person than with an anxious person.) That kind of hope does help determine the way we view ourselves in even the worst of circumstances. Hope helps us hang onto the most important elements of our character when sufferings try us in severe ways.

The Book of Hebrews helps us understand how incredibly strong that hope is:

> *Because God wanted to make the unchanging nature of his pur-*
> *pose very clear to the heirs of what was promised, he confirmed it*
> *with an oath. God did this so that, by two unchangeable things in*
> *which it is impossible for God to lie, we who have fled to take hold*
> *of the hope offered to us may be greatly encouraged. We have this*
> *hope as an anchor for the soul, firm and secure (Hebrews 6:17-19).*

Look at how strong this hope is. A few elements in this passage give assurance of the strength of hope. First, God has promised to back up hope with all the credentials of His own godliness. He is an unchanging God; therefore, what we know to be true of Him will always remain true of Him. Not only has He made promises to His people, but He has made these promises secure by taking an oath.

In earlier verses we can see that the strength of the oath comes from God's standing by all that is entailed in His being—His power, knowledge, and existence; His holiness, righteousness, goodness, justice, and truth. He supports His promises with the full force of all that He is. That won't change.

As if that is not enough, the writer then reminds us that "it is impossible for God to lie." No wonder we should be encouraged as we "take hold of the hope offered to us"! If we need encouragement, we should grab hold of hope.

The author then uses the picture of the anchor. An anchor is used to keep a boat in one position in spite of everything else that happens. What better picture of possible instability can you come up with than that of a boat on the high sea, especially with the primitive nautical equipment of the day in which Hebrews was written? It could have been treacherous to be out of sight of land in stormy weather. The anchor would have been the only stabilizing force as it held the boat in place.

The picture of the soul being anchored by hope is very graphic. Trouble can throw us around mercilessly and have us completely off course if we don't have something to hold us to a firm position of stability. The rocks may seem to be our fate if we can't get a grip of something firm.

This passage of Scripture was what first made me curious about the important strength of hope. At first I would have expected faith rather than hope to be called an "anchor for the soul." Then I began to see that we can't even get to a position of faith without first having the anchor of hope holding us steady in those confusing times when we are tossed around like a little boat in a storm. Faith is either a position of commitment or action. There are times in our lives when commitment seems beyond our grasp and action utterly impossible. Hope offers a possibility when there doesn't seem to be one at all.

Of the many examples we could examine, let me suggest a somewhat peculiar example of a tried and a persevering hope. I say it is a peculiar example because it does not end in an apparent victory; it seems to end in utter defeat. In all ways it looks as if a life was destroyed needlessly.

The story is well-known, but when we think of it, our attention is usually on the events or characters of the two better known personalities, David and Bathsheba.

Let's briefly review the story. From the wall of the palace David sees a beautiful woman bathing. He arranges to have her come to meet him, whereupon they are involved in an adulterous relationship. David then manipulates the death of her husband on the battlefield and later marries Bathsheba, who bears him a son. Nathan then speaks for God in condemning David's actions. This, in short, is the story that we usually examine.

Rarely do we look at Uriah, the victim of Bathsheba's unfaithfulness and David's murderous heart. We really don't know much about Uriah, but what little we see of him in this passage of Scripture we must admire. He is a faithful, loyal servant of the king.

Uriah was a Hittite. At that time the Hittites were one of the conquered people's of Israel. The Hittites had their own gods. We don't know whether or not Uriah followed the God of Israel, but he was a part of the army of the people that God called His very own. From all we can see, Uriah was fiercely loyal to both his soldiers and his superiors.

For some reason unknown to Uriah, the king calls him home from the battlefield. We can only speculate about what his thoughts were. This strange calling to an audience with the king probably had his mind racing with questions. Was he in trouble or was he being promoted? Either way, what had he done that had captured the attention of the king?

Maybe I am just naturally suspicious, but if it were me, I would question the purpose of such a visit, especially after the visit of David. What is recorded of the conversation offers no clear purpose from Uriah's perspective for being called—no promotion, no rebuke. Why then did the king call?

Maybe Uriah had some idea that things weren't right. Maybe there was something in Bathsheba's actions, though we could get the idea that he may not have even seen her. Maybe people were talking, or maybe something about David himself possibly caused Uriah to question— then again, maybe not. He may have been absolutely without a clue to the events, although certainly those around must have had some idea of what had taken place. How can you keep the events surrounding a king's palace quiet?

Whatever the case may be, Uriah's response is what marks him as a man of high principle. He chooses to sleep at the entrance of the palace rather than go to his own home. He chooses to suffer lack of comfort for principle.

David can't believe what Uriah has done. When David asks Uriah why he didn't go home, we see the response of a loyal man. He is loyal to the ark of God; loyal to the soldiers; and loyal to David, his king. The nation was at war, and everyone else was suffering hardship. How could he not identify with them? It wouldn't be fair.

Uriah stands in stark contrast to David's present weakness. Many years before, David had burst onto the national scene when Goliath and the Philistines challenged the Israelites. The burning question in his heart was, "Is there not a cause?" Uriah, in a sense, is asking the same thing. David had been called "a man after God's own heart" as God looked for a replacement for Saul. Now his heart is darkened with his sin as Uriah is reminding him of the purpose or cause at hand.

Uriah hangs on to a sense of purpose and remains loyal to all. God had a mandate for His people and Uriah was a part of that. Though people were not true to him, he was true to the higher purpose of God.

It is hard to hold onto hope at times, but what or who is our hope in anyway? If we have a misplaced hope, we will have a misplaced faith and a misplaced love too. We need to be sure that our hope is in God.

People will let us down. We can count on that as surely as we can count on the sun's coming up in the East. Even more sure is the fact that we can count on God and His promises to us. One day the sun will fail to rise in the East, but God will never fail.

The failure of leadership does not give us the right to be disloyal to them. It gives us the opportunity to check the placement of our hope and make sure it is in the God who is above all. Principles are greater than personalities.

Uriah is a perfect example of a man who got a raw deal and yet unflinchingly remained true to the end. His wife had committed adultery. His king had sinned against God, his wife, and him, and then manipulated events, hid the truth, and arranged for his murder. His commander, obeying orders knowingly, sent him to the worst of the battle to die. Uriah was clearly a victim.

> ### "Even more sure is the fact that we can count on God and His promises to us. One day the sun will fail to rise in the East, but God will never fail."

Everyone and everything Uriah had believed in and been faithful and loyal to, turned on him. Yet this man would not allow himself to be disloyal to God's people nor to God's cause in any way even to death. His hope was in something beyond natural sight. Certainly everything he could see seemed to be against him.

It is hard to have hope when all you have ever trusted, outside of God himself, seems to be—or maybe actually is—against you. It is absolutely essential that we put our hope in God. That is the only hope that is eternally and totally reliable, even when we do not have a discernible response from God.

In such times it is not so much that we must maintain an attitude of hope to get us through; rather hope maintains us through the harshest of life's circumstances, keeping sight of what the truly important things of life in Christ are. Those things are bigger than this mortal life we live.

Let us further consider how reliable that hope is even though disaster seems to prove otherwise.

Living in a place like Bangladesh for several years, we have become all too familiar with disaster. Floods, cyclones, and famine are recurring events, but they are all related to an earthly existence. Only one true disaster relates to us in an eternal setting, the disaster brought on by the rejection of Jesus as Lord and Savior. The disaster of an eternal hell is more than anyone would want to face. Scripture is too descriptive of this disaster for anyone to ignore.

Disasters dramatically affect the lives of those who are directly touched by them or who have come close to being a victim. Eternity eventually affects everyone. If we truly believe in the two alternatives of eternity, then logically it should drastically affect our earthly attitudes. Choices need to be made to avert disaster. We should be willing to take no risk that would lead to the disaster of an eternity in hell. Furthermore, what issue is big enough to dissuade us from eternity with the Lord?

The heaven and hell issue is much bigger than fire insurance and mansions. There is a whole life-style that develops in the "here and now" in direct relationship with what we believe about our future eternal "then and there" relationship with God.

How would you live your life if you were absolutely sure there was no eternal state for man? Some say they would still live it in the pattern of Jesus. While that is admirable, I'm not sure it is truthful.

If all that was provided in our existence were these few years on earth, I think I would do everything I could to make this life as pleasurable and as long-lasting as possible. I would, no doubt, take every advantage I could get by with, legally or otherwise. Morality wouldn't make much sense.

If there were no eternity, I think I would want to be in absolute control of everything about my life—maybe even my own death. After all, if it got to the point that pain was unbearable as well as inescapable, and death was imminent, then why not make a choice to end the pain? Euthanasia could be a sensible alternative if there were no life after this life.

"How would you live your life if you were absolutely sure there was no eternal state for man?"

Abortion would also make sense if there were no eternity, because the unborn child would not make an eternal difference. Why bring into this world a child who was not convenient? Why allow a potentially deformed fetus to live? Would these not be practical considerations if there were a lack of an eternal state? Why would any human life have value? Value, or worth, demands a comparison. When a person gets to the point that he is the most important thing in his value system, everything else is compared to himself. If the value of life is only a personal consideration for a limited period of time, then the logical goal of life would be self-indulgence. Anything else would be utterly senseless.

Suicide would also be an option for those who just didn't want to go on. What would it matter? Why would it be a tragedy if a person chose to end it all now or later if eternity were not a factor?

Strangely enough, even hell has an aspect of hope attached to it. Think about it. In the promise of hell there is at least something to look forward to. The idea of an eternal hell is certainly negative and not at all what we normally consider hopeful. Many people boldly acknowledge that they are going to hell. There is more hope for them though than for those who think or live as though there is no eternity. Those who acknowledge hell are, in an odd way, also acknowledging God. Even in that very negative sense, the hope exists that there is a God. It may be small, but it is there. A person who can have the negative hope of hell could also accept the positive hope of heaven.

The greater tragedy is for those who see mankind as their ultimate answer. With humanity as the ultimate answer, the logical end is despair. Hope says there is something more; despair says there is nothing more. When anyone comes to grips with the idea that there is no more, true desperation sets in. Desperation is a true drain on life. Desperation sees no way out, nothing good, no possibilities, no light at the end of the tunnel.

What good would it be to be humanitarian if there were no eternity? We would be saving people's lives and improving their conditions for what purpose? Despair? Despair is the antithesis of hope. With no hope for eternity, all that is left is despair.

The person who does not accept eternity is a desperate person. He is in danger every time a tragedy occurs because tragedy is a threat to such a person's very existence.

The story is quite different for those who accept the biblical truth that Jesus has gone to prepare a place for us that we might be with Him forever. For those who have accepted the great assurance that is given in the knowledge of such an eternal Savior, there is no real tragedy in life as it relates to the individual's earthly or eternal position. Salvation and the promise of eternity with the Lord are an anchor of hope that can maintain us through any calamity of life.

It is little wonder then that the expectancy of the coming of the Lord for the saints of God is called our "blessed hope."

Recall some situation where you wanted to get across a message or description to someone and no matter how hard you tried, you did not seem to get through to the person. You will quickly remember then the frustration that comes with trying to get such a point across. That is the kind of frustration I feel at times when trying to understand why the hope of heaven eludes people. · That hope seems so compelling to me and absolutely clear.

It seems to me that with such a hope, nonbelievers would eagerly and enthusiastically be turning to such a sure promise with great anticipation. It also seems to me that with such a clear hope, believers should live more hopefully above difficult circumstances. However, though we believers "should," we don't always, do we? As clear as it may seem to us, literally billions of people have not seen that there is hope. What a tragedy! In fact, it has to be the greatest tragedy: billions of people who have not caught hold of hope in Jesus as an anchor for life and eternity.

Who is really the victim: Uriah, who sees clearly the deeper purpose and will not turn away even to his own hurt, or David, who should know better but gets his eyes off of the purpose of our hope? The eternal purposes of God grant us the gift of hope even though this world may victimize us.

Are you tossed on the high seas of turmoil? Are you a victim of great injustice and maybe even senseless brutality? Or are you a victim of your own inability to see the solid value of eternal principles beyond the temporary blast of the waves of despair. I can offer you an anchor of hope. And as strong as this hope is, maybe you can see that it is enough to get you through the storm without giving in to the senselessness of despair. Hope is our anchor.

CHAPTER TWO

Not So Far From Faith

Before we talk much more about hope, let's look at faith. A great deal has been written and said about faith. Truly, I want to be a person of faith. I am sure you also want the same thing. To be honest though, I am often intimidated by faith healers and people who pray for great miracles and provisions and seem to receive them on a regular basis. I have often felt spiritually inadequate as I compare myself to such people. At times I feel like a minor-league Christian who can't quite pitch, bat, or field well enough to be in the faith big leagues.

I believe in healing and praying for the sick in faith. I also believe God still does miracles, and He gives special blessings to His people. I've seen miracles and healings. Sometimes God seems to honor my faith for such things, and sometimes the answer seems to be tabled until a future meeting.

I am like so many others who would love to have a special "faith formula" that sees miraculous works 100 percent of the time. I don't. I would also like to have a faith that is unshakable, never doubts or fears, but is always solid. I can't say I'm batting a thousand in that area either.

I feel more like one of the disciples when he heard Jesus' teachings and blurted out, "Increase our faith," because he realized how small their faith was. Jesus responded with the story of the mustard seed, letting the disciples know that a great amount of faith isn't necessary.

Faith just needs to be the right kind of seed planted in the right kind of soil; out of this, wonderful things grow.

I'm not writing these things because I think I have new, great answers. I'm writing because I have had great questions that quite possibly are like yours. Where does faith come from, and how can we appropriate it for ourselves? Is faith only for success and prosperity, or is it for the hard times too?

Let's dig deep down to a rock solid faith. If you are like me, you are getting sick of all the religious exaggerations and empty formulas. I regularly face problems, big problems. In those hard times I need answers of encouragement. In such times I'm not concerned about casting mountains into seas. I am concerned about surviving the storm.

"Where does faith come from, and how can we appropriate it for ourselves?"

We need to be people of faith. Sometimes, however, the tests are so new or so big or so hard that we aren't sure we even have what it takes to have faith. This book is really written for those whose mettle is being tested or who are being bashed about like an anchorless, small ship in a huge raging sea. Maybe faith doesn't even seem like a possibility for you at this point, but how about hope? Does hope seem more within your reach?

I've never heard anyone say he wants to be a "man of hope." We admire a "man of faith" and desire to be such a person. Our goal is faith, but in the process of becoming people of deep faith, hope is so important that we cannot continue to overlook it. Since faith is a goal, let's see how we can get there, and what will keep us through the trials along the way.

First, let us distinguish between two kinds of faith; passive faith and active faith. Both are very important. Without some distinction between the two, though, we can get bogged down in our understanding of what faith is and what we do with faith.

"Passive" is not to be understood as wimpy and weak. I am using the word *passive* because there is that aspect of our faith that doesn't require any outward action on our part beyond belief and trust. This is faith in that full set of Bible promises and principles upon which we base our trust. It is the kind of faith whereby we can say, "I have faith in God." This kind of faith is very broad and very necessary. We begin here because it is foundational to all that follows. In fact, we really can't continue on without it because "without faith it is impossible to please God" (Hebrews 11:6).

This aspect of faith is something you can have, and it becomes a quality of your being. You are first a person of faith as you trust in God and His Word. Do you believe God? Even a little bit? If so, great! The rest grows from the smallest childlike trust in Him. If you haven't yet been able to believe in God and His promises, don't you at least hope He is there and able to help you? Let that hope lead you to faith. I think you may find you have much more faith than you think.

Active faith then is something we do. We can believe that healing is biblical, and yet possibly nothing happens. There is that side of active faith, though, that works the works of God in our present circumstances to accomplish His purposes. These are acts of a supernatural miraculous nature.

With these two understandings of faith, you can imagine the resulting difficulties if we put emphasis on one to the exclusion or near exclusion of the other. Yet, some people do. We need both types of faith in our lives, the trusting passive faith as well as the active faith. We also need a balance of faith.

Those who have an unbalanced desire for active faith may not concern themselves with building a greater trusting relationship with God. Such people tend to want the spectacular and often fail to see the importance of building personal character and a personal relationship with God. Such people tend to be more interested in the active gifts of the Spirit rather than in the character building fruit of the Spirit.

On the other hand those who are not interested in the gifts of the Spirit either relegate them to the past or don't see a need for them now. Unfortunately, these are often people who tend to be skeptical of the supernatural manifestations of God. Or possibly they simply don't understand how such manifestations can work in their own lives.

We must have a balance between passive and active faith. I want the fruit of the Spirit in my life because I am growing in the faith. I also want to see the manifestations of the Spirit by faith. Both areas of faith present challenges of growth that I have not fully achieved yet. If I can first be a man of faith, then I believe God will also honor the actions I do in faith.

It seems to me that more of us have misunderstandings about having works of faith than about being a person of faith. The problem I have is that God cannot always honor the act I thought I did in faith. I am sometimes presumptuous. Sometimes I get in the way with wrong motives or I misunderstand what God's purposes are and respond incorrectly, especially in the hard, tricky cases.

> **"The strength of my faith is…not dependent on my ability to exercise faith, but it is in the assurance that the One in whom I put my faith will not fail."**

Though God may not always honor the acts I may have thought were acts of faith, He will always honor the trusting faith that I have put in Him. The strength of my faith is then not dependent on my ability to exercise faith, but it is in the assurance that the One in whom I put my faith will not fail.

So what happens when God does not respond as I thought He should? If faith is truly a part of my being, and through belief I have given Him the right in my life to be the God that He is, then I should not give in to the temptation to complain against Him. Nor should I be devastated because things didn't work the way I thought they were supposed to. It should not damage my relationship with God if I pray for a person and the person is not healed. God is not under obligation to work according to my definition of faith. I am under obligation, however, to remain a person who has fixed his very existence by faith in God.

Here are a couple of biblical accounts to underscore the strength of what I have said so far. First, let's look at the three Hebrews in the fiery furnace. They had faith! You know the story: Shadrach, Meshach, and Abednego would not compromise their faith in God and bow down to worship an idol. King Nebuchadnezzar was furious when he heard that his order had not been obeyed. The Hebrews' faith could not be compromised. Peer pressure could not get them to bow, nor could threats of death from a notoriously cruel despot like Nebuchadnezzar cause them to bow to an idol.

I love the answer they gave to the king when he challenged them to face their own death if they disobeyed. Their faith was deeper than any action they could have performed. Their faith was in the unseeable reality of God. Their act of faith was their open proclamation of what God would do for them. Let's look at their defense.

The Bible account doesn't name the spokesman for the three; they were evidently equally clear in their position and response. To Nebuchadnezzar they boldly said:

> *We do not defend ourselves before you in this matter. If we are thrown into the blazing furnace, the God we serve is able to save us from it, and he will rescue us from your hand, O king. But even if he does not, we want you to know, O king, that we will not serve your gods or worship the image of gold you have set up (Daniel 3:16-18).*

Notice three statements made based on the faith that Shadrach, Meshach, and Abednego had in a God they had never seen.

First, they said, "The God we serve is able to save us." Our faith in God says that He *can* act on our behalf. God is powerful enough. In fact, He is the Almighty God. All power is His. No power can win over Him. Any other power is subject to Him. He does not share power with an evil opposite force. Remember, the devil had to request permission to even touch Job.

God does have the ability to save us. He is powerful enough to heal. He can deliver us from dilemma. The possibility of powerfully overruling any situation is within the realm of God's limitless ability. God can.

These three men sensed God's able power. They took that next step beyond mere knowledge of a passive stated fact. They boldly declared that "he will rescue us from your hand, O king." This could easily be called an act of faith. They had no way of knowing what God really would do. There was no prophetic word to them, no handwritten message on any wall, no written record of what steps God takes when faced with furnaces, nothing! They had nothing except an awareness of the love God has for His people of faith in times of trouble. They had faith enough to say "God *will*."

Wow! What powerful faith. What men of faith they were to be able to say with such assurance that God *can* and God *would* act on their behalf.

If the story stopped here, I would most likely fall into a depression. In my experience, even though I know the Almighty God can do great things for me and that He will do great things for me as I exercise my faith, He does not always do everything I want or need simply upon my proclamation.

Here is the problem. Even though God can and God will, He doesn't always perform according to what I think is an act of faith. The problem is not with God, it's with me. At times I forget that God is not obligated to be obedient to my will or wish; I am obligated to Him.

Look at the rest of the furnace faith. Shadrach, Meshach, and Abednego did not stop with knowing that God can and God will act on their behalf; they went an important step further. This may be the most crucial part of faith. Carefully consider their insight on the gangplank to a fiery furnace. Feel their faithful defiance undergirded with eternal assurance as they look the most powerful threat they have ever known squarely in the eye and continue to reply, "But even if he does not, we want you to know, O king, that we will not serve your gods or worship the image of gold you have set up."

"But…if…not!" What do they mean, but *if not!* I know God is the Almighty. That takes away my fear of powerful people and problems. I know God will help me. That reassures me that I have a power available that includes the miraculous. If God does not act in my time of trial in a spectacular rescue operation, the real strength of my faith is that it really doesn't matter. "If not," I will still serve Him. No devil can change that. My faith is not in what He will do when I act in faith. My faith is in who He is. I worship Him with or without the demonstration of the miraculous or the fine provisions that can come from the hand of God. If those things are there, I will enjoy them. If not, I will still serve Him.

Basically that's the attitude of Paul, a man in prison in chains as he writes the Book of Philippians. He says, "I know what it is to be in need, and I know what it is to have plenty. I have learned the secret of being content in any and every situation, whether well fed or hungry, whether living in plenty or in want" (Philippians 4:11-12).

Remember, this is the man who gives us a partial list of his problems, which not only includes being in prison for his faith on numerous occasions but also being flogged, exposed to death, beaten five times with thirty-nine strikes of a whip, beaten with rods three times, stoned, shipwrecked three times, as well as facing dangerous rivers, bandits, people who sought to hurt him, hunger, thirst, cold, and at times going without proper clothes.

If these are the acts of a man of faith, then it is a faith in a different dimension than the reportedly powerful, victorious, conquering exploits that imply the best of health, the finest of facilities, and the adoration of the majority.

Faith is powerful. It is victorious, and men of faith do conquering exploits through God's power. But there is another side of faith that puts up with the ugly realities of living in a sin-saturated world. Such faith has an inward conquest not always visible or noticeable. People of faith do get cancer. People of faith do suffer disaster. The faith of the faithful will be challenged, and God will even allow the challenge. But like Paul's faith in the prison chains, our faith in God is not based on whether or not we are abounding with blessings or being abased with this world's abuses, because "I can do everything through him who gives me strength" (Philippians 4:13).

Which things? All things. That means the good as well as the bad. The kind of faith I need lasts through it all—absolutely all. Anything less allows me just enough room to fear and doubt.

Let's be realistic without being pessimistic. We are going to have troubles. No need to deny it. No need to sugarcoat it with positive superstatements of confidence. As long as we are living on this sin-polluted planet, we are going to face troubles in varying degrees. Some people will have minor difficulties. Others will have mind-boggling messes. But all will at some time face ugly challenges.

We do need to be positive, but it must be a positiveness that goes deep into the soul. How do we develop positive responses to negative situations? That seems to be one of our bigger problems. The answers come through the testing of our responses. I take great comfort in this Scripture verse:

> *No temptation has seized you except what is common to man. And God is faithful; he will not let you be tempted beyond what you can bear. But when you are tempted, he will also provide a way out so that you can stand up under it (1 Corinthians 10:13).*

With every problem comes a temptation. God clearly does not allow things to come our way that we cannot bear. So if He knows what I can handle and has given written assurances, then I can confidently face such problems and the subsequent temptations. I can survive and even win over the debilitating depression that often comes from the effects of problems.

If I am not careful, I can allow my negative circumstances to make me think something is wrong with me. If I am living in sin, then something is wrong with me; I need salvation. However, I am addressing here believers who face the same "rain" of troubles that fall on "the righteous and the unrighteous" (Matthew 5:45). Believers do have problems. How do we apply faith to our problems?

Maybe past or current experiences of defeat and the feelings of helplessness are making you want to quit, to give up on everything. Possibly, at the moment it is difficult for you to agree that you can make it through the turmoil. If discouragement has brought you to a place where you are finding it difficult to accept that your situation will improve, could you at least try to agree with me on the cold logic of being able to have conquering faith in all things? It really does make sense even if your feelings are making things seem senseless and hopeless. Possibly you feel like Charlie Brown in the comic strip. Charlie Brown is obviously depressed after another terrible defeat where he pitched poorly for his team. Someone comes up to him and says, "Well, you win some and you lose some." Charlie Brown replies, "Wouldn't that be neat?"

It's hard to be a person of faith when everything seems to be against us. Let's look at an extreme test case: Job. Job was a man of faith who had a bad day, a *really* bad day. To start with, God *allows* the devil to bring all manner of havoc into Job's life at the same time. Enemies attack on one front and kill all but one servant who returns to report that the whole herd of donkeys and oxen were stolen. From another direction another sole-surviving servant comes only to say that fire has fallen, and all the flocks are gone.

The next lone survivor comes from still another field to report that other enemies have killed workers and have stolen all the camels. Then coming from the home of Job's oldest son, a final messenger appears to bring the worst news yet: a wind had blown the corners of his son's house down, and all of his sons and daughters were killed.

That bad day is followed by still another devastatingly bad day. This time Job has sores all over his body, not to mention a nagging wife and three critical friends! Remember, this was all *allowed* by God.

Then Job makes an incredible but very quotable statement, "Though he [God] slay me, yet will I *hope* in him" (Job 13:15, emphasis added).

That is the kind of faith I am talking about—faith for the tough stuff. Notice that this great man of faith expresses himself in the middle of his problems through an unseen hope.

This is the kind of faith we see in Hebrews 11, known as the faith chapter. The first half of the chapter looks at heroes who are like the heroes we know. These are the biblical Rambo types who did great, heroic things for God. The second half of the chapter, though, tells of those who endured all manner of troubles and yet are still in the list of heroes.

Some of us may be in the first half of the chapter. Such people are blessed and are a great inspiration. So many more of us, though, seem to be in the second half: life is tough. And at times it seems there is nothing to show for it, no "trophies" of the struggle. Yet the promise of the glory of God is equal for all of us.

I want to be a man of great faith, a strong, enduring, deep, unshakable faith. I want the kind of faith that goes beyond the fanfare. The fanfare is thrilling, but most people do not receive the adulation of the crowds or have their names printed in ecclesiastical headlines. Most need a faith to carry them through an untimely death, a long, debilitating illness, financial despair, endless days in anonymity doing the best they can, or any of a host of this life's challenges.

I want that kind of faith, don't you? I want a faith that will stand strong through the test. But how do we get such faith? First, we need hope. A strong faith is built with a strong hope. Hope is not a lazy substitute for faith; it is usually preparatory to faith. It is the undergirding of faith.

A position of hope seems easier to reach than faith. On the surface it seems that it would not be difficult to become a man of hope. Faith seems more intimidating. When I can understand the close relationship between faith and hope, then I am encouraged. If I can just get enough courage to hope as Job did, then maybe I am not so far from faith.

CHAPTER THREE

Springing from Hope

Faith, hope, and love are three important elements of our Christian life. We find them listed together at the end of 1 Corinthians 13, which is known as the love chapter.

After dealing with so many sticky issues in the Corinthian church and following the important teachings on the Lord's Supper, spiritual gifts, and the unity of the body of Christ, these three stand out as essential building blocks for successful Christian lives. Others have called them the three graces. No matter what you choose to call them, I get the strongest impression from Paul that when the smoke clears and the weaker unimportant things in our lives have been shot down, these three should still be standing, alive and strong.

Among the three, love unquestionably gets top billing in the Corinthian account, and of course faith is famous. It's that other one—hope—that we seldom consider seriously in connection with spiritual things. Yet hope is sprinkled throughout Scripture in such important ways.

Hope comes up in our conversations a lot, but usually it is thought of as little more than a cosmic chance. The common variety of hope is very easy to attain. Most people have no trouble thinking hopefully when it is merely wishful thinking.

Perhaps you already know the story about the boy sitting with his line in the water, fishing. An older fisherman in passing greeted him in the universal fisherman's greeting, "Have you caught any?" Without a moment's thought, the boy replied, "Well, if I catch this one that's nibbling and another two, I'll have three!" I'm like that little boy and not ashamed of it. I know I'm not alone. Probably you find this kind of hope comes easy too.

There is no end to my hope in these terms. I hope for everything. I hope it doesn't rain when I must be out. I hope it does rain when it would cancel any program I don't really want to go to. I hope my salary goes up and my expenses go down. I hope for a white Christmas but no other white days at all if I have to drive. I hope my hometown Kansas City Royals win when every time they play I hope my investments grow and gas prices go down. I hope we have tacos tonight for supper with strawberry shortcake for dessert, and I hope I won't add any more to the spare tire around my waist when I eat it.

Do you see what I mean? All the little things I hope for are endless. I don't just hope for little things, though. I hope for big things, too, even spiritual things at times.

I hope that my children will live happy, successful Christian lives with loving spouses for as many years as God gives them. I hope for peace in this world even though I know it will not come until the end of the age brings about the Millennium. I hope that the sick people we pray for will be healed soon. I hope that there will be a sweeping move of God that would usher millions into the Kingdom from all around the world.

A hopeful attitude can be very effortless for most people. The wish list, a daydream-like kind of hope, is especially easy. We talk of exerting our faith, but we never talk about the exercise of hope. Faith seems to take a great deal of effort. Some of the answers for our faith come only by fasting and prayer. It's not easy to fast and pray. Although we talk about works of faith, we don't seem to need works of hope. Yet, as we will see more clearly, hope is a prerequisite for faith.

Is hope a wishful daydream? If so, I'm fortunate. It takes little effort for me to come up with ideas of things that would make my life easier or more pleasant or to wish my situation were enhanced or eased. However, I don't think this kind of hope, in such a common usage of the word, is what will satisfy our prerequisite of faith.

The kind of hope I need is not made of daydreams. Nor is this hope personal hype, where we pump up our emotions. This kind of hope is not an imaginary wish that suddenly comes true almost magically by a mysterious faith that puts flesh on dreams. Instead, hope is that encouragement to trust the very real God and His promises.

In Scripture there seems to be a definite relationship between faith, hope, and love whereby each helps to support the other. Without hope in our lives it is difficult to see faith and love. How can you even have faith without first having hope? Hope is the possibility of that which seems impossible, and faith is the assurance that it is or will be. I would be afraid of someone with faith if he were not tempered with love.

"Hope is the possibility of that which seems impossible, and faith is the assurance that it is or will be."

One of the places where we see the importance of hope in relationship to the other members of the big three is in the Book of Colossians where Paul talks about "the faith and love that spring from the hope that is stored up for you in heaven" (Colossians 1:5).

Knowing that love and faith spring from hope helps me. Faith can seem so difficult, and I know I am not always as loving as I should be. But I rarely have a difficult time hoping. Since hope is already "user friendly," I want to have the right kind of hope that will lead me to the right kind of faith and love.

The kind of hope that leads to faith is the kind that reassures the intuitive knowledge in everyone that God exists and that He is working on our behalf. Have you ever noticed that you just know some things? No one had to tell you, you just intuitively knew. Some of our most basic understanding of God is like that. We just know He is there. There are no true atheists in the world; they are all backsliders, denying what is built inside: a simple knowledge that there is a God. All people sense that God exists. Faith is putting our trust in such a God. It is the hope that grows out of this intuition that first helps us to accept God by faith.

Hope also provides the possibility that we can see great changes in our lives as we act upon our faith in God. Hope says it is possible; faith says it is sure.

The kind of hope I am advocating is made of truth. Truth either is completely true, or it isn't truth at all. Truth is eternal and never changes. It can withstand all tests. Such truth is only in the God who reveals himself to our hearts and who is more fully revealed in the Bible. Even the simplest of hope based in Him is sure. The bedrock of hope is the truth of the unchangeable, eternal God whom we have known intuitively from the beginning.

The hope of truth always precedes the acceptance of truth. Hope, in anticipation, sees truth with its possibilities. It presents those possibilities for examination and they in turn are accepted as real and worthy of our commitment in faith. Bedrock hope leads to bedrock faith.

Hope can lead us to love. It seems natural. Hope and hate just don't make sense together. One builds, the other destroys. But hope and love are hand and glove. Love is full of hope. We want the best for ourselves and for those we love.

Again let us begin with the foundations. God is love. To have strong, loving relationships, we must begin with a loving relationship with the very source of love, God himself.

Many people have trouble at this point. Either they don't believe in God or they live as though there is not a loving God.

Many people are skeptical about the love of God. Those who suffer often are skeptical of a God who is capable of loving them totally and unconditionally. Those who are in despair find His love difficult to enjoy. Tough circumstances can deceive us into believing that God is impersonal or at least silent when it comes to our own problems. In the hard times we are often tempted to ask, "Where is the loving God?"

As you search for the relationship of hope and love in Scripture, you will see the verses in the Book of Psalms that link hope with God's unfailing love. The Bible presents a God who by His very nature does not give up in His commitment to us. He never fails to do the loving best thing for us.

God's commitment to eternal love is a tremendous truth. Just think of the hope wrapped up in the knowledge of having the unchanging God loving us always. He's not going to quit. He won't walk out on us. He won't turn a deaf ear when we need a hearing. No matter how badly we messed it up this time, He is still there to accept us.

"The Bible presents a God who by His very nature does not give up in His commitment to us."

We may fail God, but He will never fail us. This is difficult for many of us to understand. Through our experiences with people we may have learned that when we fail others, they reject or fail us. This is not true with God. He is always extending His love to us. We can always count on His readiness to love us in the best way.

"So I tell you, every sin and blasphemy will be forgiven men, but the blasphemy against the Spirit will not be forgiven" (Matthew 12:31). Possibly when you first look at these words, they don't seem to speak of the unfailing love of God. They appear to be unforgiving and judgmental. The tone of the message doesn't seem to be one of unconditional love and acceptance. It seems that if we fail God, then He will fail us. There's not much hope or love in that idea. Let us not misunderstand. Many of our problems with God are simply that, our misunderstanding of Him.

This Scripture verse used to scare me because I misunderstood it. People had always told me that blasphemy against the Holy Spirit was the unpardonable sin. No one really has ever had to tell me what sin is. I've always known. So have you. We know when we do wrong. No one ever had to give me sin lessons either. I found that I was a natural. I picked it up without having to practice. Doing wrong is still too easy. If sin is failing God, then you and I both have a big problem—especially if there is one kind of sin that is unpardonable.

Blasphemy is a religious word that we don't deal with every day. Blasphemy is, in short, insulting God by word or action. When I understood the concept of blasphemy, then I was afraid that maybe I had already said something or sometime in the future would say or do something that offends the Holy Spirit and could never be forgiven. I knew of specific things I had done that were insulting to the holy God. I further reasoned that if God couldn't forgive me, then He would no longer have any love for me.

I've met other people who have said they were so bad that God couldn't love them because they had sinned too much and were beyond hope even for God. I know many people must feel this way. They have great mountains of guilt because they know that they have done wrong and don't know how to be forgiven or how to conquer the wrong that they do so easily. We make matters worse by cutting off the God of love from our lives.

God's love is so great that we cannot escape it. There is no place we can go where He cannot reach us. There hasn't been a person born who is bad enough to be beyond the reach of the love of God.

What is this unpardonable sin then? Unfortunately, those who take on a blasphemous or insulting approach to God create difficulties for themselves. They have put themselves in an unpardonable position. It's not that God can't or won't forgive them, but rather they refuse to be pardoned. God has given us His love unreservedly. It is mankind who rejects God's love. God does not reject people's desire to love Him.

Jesus is God's greatest expression of His love to mankind. It is the work of the Holy Spirit to draw men to Jesus. There is no person on earth that the Holy Spirit is not trying to draw to Jesus. Therefore, if we reject the Spirit of God who is trying to bring us to God's love, how can there be forgiveness? We would have refused the very one who would introduce us to Jesus, the one God gave to all the world as an expression of His greatest love.

If God hasn't rejected us, but rather we have rejected Him, then there is clearly the possibility of obtaining a hope that God loves us unconditionally and unfailingly. Think about it. If God is true and if He is love, as the Bible says, then isn't it possible that any sin of ours can be forgiven? Forgiveness is possible as long as we don't reject the love of God given for us through His Son Christ Jesus.

Love springs in our hearts from such a hope. Just think of the possibilities because the eternal, Almighty God loves us.

Some of our greatest struggles in life center around our relationships of faith and love. There is great risk in either of these two areas.

Some of your hardest times may be related to disappointments in one of these areas. Possibly a venture begun in full faith has failed. You were left confused and questioning. Or perhaps you have had your love bruised or rejected; you fear the risk of loving again. If so, maybe you need to build a strong hope, because "faith and love...spring from hope."

CHAPTER FOUR

You're Gonna Make It

Colossians has told us that faith and love spring from hope. But where does hope spring from? Are you ready for the answer to this one? It's not an easy answer at all, but it is a good one. It is found in Romans 5:1-5:

> *Since we have been justified through faith, we have peace with God through our Lord Jesus Christ, through whom we have gained access by faith into this grace in which we now stand. And we rejoice in the hope of the glory of God. Not only so, but we also rejoice in our sufferings, because we know that suffering produces perseverance; perseverance, character; and character, hope. And hope does not disappoint us, because God has poured out his love into our hearts by the Holy Spirit, whom he has given us.*

Hope comes from Jesus. You probably anticipated that part of the answer. Jesus, by His grace, saves us when we put our faith in Him. Therefore we can rejoice in two things, both of which are hopeful in nature. We rejoice first "in the hope of the glory of God," but we also can rejoice "in our sufferings." It is through suffering that we develop perseverance which produces character which produces a hope that is saturated with the love of God that the Holy Spirit gives.

Wow! This hope we have is not flimsy stuff! A person of character who has been under the dealings of God and has the hope that God puts in him can build an ark or part a sea or do some other spectacular thing. Let's not try to bill ourselves as people of faith and yet neglect the foundation of a solid hope that produces a solid faith. Look at this progression. It begins with suffering.

I am not advocating self-inflicted sufferings, nor do I want to exalt suffering simply for suffering's sake in our lives. Those are extremes. The denial of suffering or equating suffering with a lack of faith is also extreme. The reality is that suffering in varying degrees occurs in our lives. We can work through it and be made stronger with Christ's help. We can accept that which the devil meant for our discouragement and destruction and allow it to produce greater hope instead.

From the little exposure I have had to Judo, I notice an underlying principle in many of the Judo movements. The opponent's own weight and the force of his assault are used to throw the opponent to the mat. That principle can also be the beauty of sufferings in our lives. We can use the force of the devil's assault to overcome him in hope. We can turn the weight of suffering thrust upon us into a positive useful force in our lives.

A good friend of mine, David Wigington, had his arm cut off above the elbow in a meat grinder when he was sixteen. I didn't meet Dave until several years later. Few people have an overcoming, outgoing attitude such as his. He has infused that same attitude into his children, who have excelled in many areas of their lives.

I noticed especially how Dave turned the potentially discouraging accident into a very positive aspect of his life. Dave wears a prosthesis. This motorized arm attracts a lot of attention, especially in a place like Bangladesh. When Dave and his family visited us, people were very curious about his bionic arm. I began to realize this is a curiosity he has to deal with all the time. The silent stares could no doubt get tiresome after years of repetition. Instead of allowing the quizzical looks to bother him, Dave uses his arm as an opportunity to make friends, to witness, or just to have fun showing people how it works and what he can do with it. I have never heard nor seen anything from Dave that indicated his arm is a problem either to him or to his family.

How can we bypass the element of suffering? How is it at all possible to deny ourselves, take up a cross to follow Jesus, and not face suffering in some way?

The cross is an instrument of death. Suffering and death are hand and glove. If I am to put to death my sinful nature on a cross, how can suffering be avoided? The sinful flesh does not die easily. Sure, I have a new spirit in me, but the flesh is still there to contend with. Killing a habit is hard. Putting thoughts under subjection can be agonizing. I can have victory through Christ Jesus, but victory does not come without a battle. No battle is waged without the element of suffering. The suffering can be physical, mental, or emotional.

Suffering produces perseverance in us. What value is the sufferings of the cross if reaching the finish is not the goal? If Jesus had come down from the cross, as those jeering mockers had suggested, the purpose of the cross would have been compromised. Such an act would not have proven His divine nature because it would have stopped short of God's purposes. Jesus persevered to the end because from the beginning He knew what God's purposes were. God's purposes clearly included the suffering of Christ.

In the same way, the Bible is clear about our perseverance. We are to fight the good fight, run the race, put our hand to the plow, not look back, stand fast, press on toward the mark, endure hardness, etc. Nietzsche said: "Was *mich nicht umbringt, macht mich stärker.*" (That which does not kill me, makes me stronger.)

A person who learns to persevere through sufferings without turning back is the kind of person who will endure to the end. The reward at the end is worth the price! The difficulty is that we can't always see the end. If fact, most of the time the end is not visible until we get there. And even then, at times, only in retrospect do we realize that the trial is over, that we made it through.

One of the influential people in my life was Charles Greenaway, our administrative supervisor on the mission field. Brother Greenaway had a very colorful personality. He used many catchy phrases that somehow were more than just simple sayings. They contained a philosophy of living and working. Among the many phrases he used, one became a motto for many of us. Over and over again he would tell us, "You're gonna make it!"

Brother Greenaway would be able to visit us only once a year, and we always presented problems that needed solving. We had been wrestling with tough situations in less than convenient circumstances in a culture far different from our own. Frustrations can build to a boiling point and one feels something just has to either blow or go. He realized he could not solve all our problems anyway, so he usually chose to encourage us instead; that was what we really needed anyway. From the beginning to the end of his time with us he kept reminding us, "You're gonna make it." Before he left, we started believing we could.

I believe as you trust God and follow Jesus "you're gonna make it" too. No matter what our circumstances are, we can persevere to the end. We know what the goal is and we know what God expects from us. We also know the Lord has done everything to make it possible for us to make it past absolutely any obstacle. Jesus has shown us the way, and the Holy Spirit has been given to help us.

We had many unusual struggles in our first four-year term on the mission field. The struggles didn't end after those first four years; instead, they became more intense. Coming back from a year's furlough, I expected things to be better in our second term. After all, we were veterans by that time. From the day we stepped off the plane, and for the next four years, we were relentlessly assaulted from every side. It seemed that every area of our lives that could be tested was tested.

The last few days of that term were capped off with such intense pressures that I was beginning to wonder how I could bear it. I just wanted to escape but couldn't. Picture the situation. We had been through four more years of mounting pressure with few results in the work. I was faced with a year of being on the road, away from my family for most of the time, with the task of sharing a vision for the work. People expect victory sermons from missionaries. We had precious few bright spots, let alone many visible, measurable victories. What was I going to say to people who had supported us for ten years?

"Jesus has shown us the way, and the Holy Spirit has been given to help us."

On top of that, we were in the frantic last moments of packing our household into a storage room across town in the middle of the hot, tropical summer with temperatures in the high 90s and humidity in the 75 to 85 percentile. Of course the air conditioner and the fans had to be taken down too.

Not only were we closing up the house, but a million details had to be nailed down before leaving the office for a year. I had to answer those who-was-going-to-do-what-and-when kind of questions.

It was in those last four or five days before furlough that I learned of the recent return of a staff member with whom I had worked for over seven years. He had stolen the equivalent of four years' worth of his salary and fled to another country. Though he could not justify what he had done, I knew his erratic actions were a result of intense family problems.

The situation was bad enough, but then other believers decided to have him put in jail. I hurt for this man whom I considered a friend and with whom I had worked so closely. Yet, I was relieved that I would not be drawn into the mess. I was wrong. I ended up deeply involved. It consumed more of my time and was a great emotional drain.

I didn't think I could get more frustrated and discouraged at that point. I was wrong again. The next day I got a call from a very powerful man in the nation asking for a meeting. The man and the meeting were too important to ignore. I had to make time for him in the middle of the ongoing chaos even though I was sure it would be another unpleasant encounter.

At our meeting the man reasserted his immovable position that had thwarted our progress for over a year. The situation was terribly discouraging. The project was already in its fourth year, and we had absolutely nothing to show for our efforts. At one point he slammed his hands on the desk stood up and screemed at me. Because of who he was it was extremely intimidating.

I left for furlough in pitiful shape. We were to take a few days of vacation on our way home. Our first stop was in Pakistan where we had a courtesy hotel accommodation, which I was looking forward to because of our state of exhaustion. Instead, a friend of a friend met us and insisted on showing us Karachi. For over six hours we toured Karachi at the unbending insistence of this previously unknown person.

Instead of getting rest, we were out so long that we had to rush to make the flight. We spent a total of fifteen minutes in the hotel room.

Then we made it to Cairo for a one day stop to see the pyramids. Some con artist of a lady had us driving in a taxi all over Cairo for a couple of hours in the wrong direction because she said it was "right on the way" to where she was going. Being unfamiliar with the city, we had agreed to share the taxi. When we realized we were headed the wrong way, we knew something was wrong. The episode ended with our getting out of the taxi and into another. The first taxi driver was pounding on our taxi yelling at us and at the lady who was trying to take both him and us "for a ride."

We left Cairo and went on to Italy where we rented a car for a few days. We tried to find a hotel that night. We went frantically from one closed door to another until we finally decided to sleep in the car. The next morning, utterly exhausted, we stopped at a gas station. There I backed the rental car into a gas pump, breaking the glass gas filter which caused the gas to pour out all over.

Next, our flight gave us a courtesy stop in Amsterdam for the night. I woke up the next morning with what I thought was indigestion. The pain grew more intense as the morning went on. I was more ready for the last leg of our journey to the States; I was not going to let pain stop me. They almost didn't allow me to go on the flight because they could see my great discomfort. I found out later it was a gallbladder attack. The second attack and subsequent operation were only a few weeks later. Then, a month after our arrival in the States, Dad died.

Maybe you've seen the stress chart that lists different stressful situations and gives a stress value number to each. According to the chart, at a certain combined score a person is in danger due to stress. I added up my score and found I was two and a half times over the danger limit!

Have you ever wanted to quit? Believe me, after all that had happened I wanted to quit. I didn't know what I wanted to quit from; I just wanted the problems to stop. I was tired of the frustrations and didn't have a good grip on the solid principles of hope.

Brother Greenaway used to tell us it wasn't wrong to quit. He said he quit every morning while shaving. He looked in the mirror, and talked to himself saying, "Why go in to work? All that's there are problems and people with problems." We all have those days. He told us, "It's not wrong to quit—as long as you go on to work!"

It is easy to quit and very hard to doggedly hang on to hope in the face of ugly circumstances. That's what perseverance is—hanging in there in spite of it all.

> **"Have you ever wanted to quit?**
> **Believe me, after all that had**
> **happened I wanted to quit. I didn't**
> **know what I wanted to quit from;**
> **I just wanted the problems to stop."**

Persevering is not a negative attitude. It is militantly victorious. We need to develop a persevering spiritual, mental attitude. It's the sort of attitude that says no amount of difficulty will make us quit. It also takes the position that the temptation to quit is too small for people like us, because we are not the kind of people who give up. When we begin to develop such an attitude, we begin to make that next progression to character.

Character is the reflection of God's moral attributes in us. Therefore, as character relates to sin, I cannot picture certain things as being a part of God's character. If it is not a part of God's character, then I should not allow it to be a part of mine. We need to remember we are children of the King. There are certain things that children of the King just do not do.

Morally, God is holy, meaning He is absolutely pure in being and in actions. He is righteous. He will always do what is right. He is also just. He will judge all fairly according to His holy, righteous standard. God is good too. All that is good comes from Him. God is true; He is genuine.

As we suffer the death of a selfish sin that doesn't want to die, as we "press toward the mark, and persevere victoriously," our character begins to take on more of the moral integrity of God himself. This is a natural growth process. We should expect to become more holy, righteous, just, good, and true. Others should expect to see these things evident in our lives. They are watching.

Look at the fruit of the Spirit in Galatians. This is a list of moral characteristics. What else would we expect to grow out of the Spirit of God in our lives? When we have identified ourselves as believers, almost everyone expects that we will become more like God in our moral character. People are skeptical of supersaints, but they are very appreciative of people of character whose actions are good and pure. The world desperately needs to see the character of God reflected in His people, especially in their actions.

This whole process of character building through spiritual fruit cultivation presupposes that we maintain an ever-growing fellowship with God. There is no way for us to become more like God without a close fellowship with Him. However, during times of suffering, it is too easy for us to develop a strained relationship with God. This doesn't happen because He has created the tension in the relationship, but because we did. It seems that when we face physical sufferings, we are tempted to question why God is allowing these things. Or when we are struggling with our fleshly desires that refuse to die easily, we wonder why God doesn't deliver us.

As we begin to overcome doubts and mature to the point of choosing to persevere rather than to succumb, our fellowship with God improves. We begin to realize how much we really want and need God. We renew and deepen our understanding of God as our sustainer as well as our deliverer. As we progress, persevering all the way, we learn more and more about God and about ourselves. In drawing closer to God we begin to see that the trials aren't all bad; we gain character lessons from them.

For instance, I have never claimed to be a patient person. My impatience has been a source of great suffering for me, and I am sure for others. I have not been like God on this issue. In fact, I have not always seen that I even needed to be! I was a prime candidate for "patience" lessons from God. I haven't graduated yet, but I am learning.

Along the way I learned a poem. It is one of the few poems I can recite, mostly because it is short and has a point with which I identify.

It goes like this:

> Patience is a virtue,
> Possess it if you can.
> Seldom found in women,
> Never found in men!

I have struggled trying to be more like God in this area of my life. I am continuing to persevere through this problem area. Along the way I am learning great lessons as I learn to fellowship with God.

Little things going wrong can drive me straight up the wall. So, little things keep going wrong. I believe God has even allowed them for my good so a character quality can be built in me.

For example, just to name a few challenges, of the eighty plus second hand computers that have been donated to the ministries in Bangladesh, all in working order to begin with, less than half are working. One worker stole hard drives, some burned up without electric protection. Of the fifty hard drives we brought to fix our computers half were taken from our luggage. Dozens of walkie talkies have either been broken or stolen. Someone decided that the surge protectors for the twelve washers and drivers would be better used in their own projects therefore all twelve machines burned up. Beyond that, we are building eight new buildings. Enough said.

There was a time when this list of everyday matters alone would have created almost enough frustration to have me committed to an institution! Character is not built overnight. It takes time in fellowship with God through a process of perseverance. Unwillingly submitting to the dealings of God produces rebellion. A willing submission produces character.

Character doesn't come easy, but it does come, and so does a solid hope. The steps from suffering to perseverance to character lead to a strong hope. A person who has been under the dealings of God and has learned that God has a purpose in all his struggles has also learned that the purpose is good—whatever it may be and whether or not it's known to him—because God is good. That is a person with a hope as solid as God himself because the hope is based on God himself. A person of character always has hope developed by persevering through sufferings.

CHAPTER FIVE

Hope from the Heart of God

Hope is not a gamble or risk. It is not built on chance. The kind of hope we have been talking about is not a lottery ticket, with maybe one chance in a few million of winning. "Chance" is not a consideration. Biblical hope is a solid expectation and anticipation of what really can happen. It has substance, not just wishful thinking. It is also full of the purposes of God for our lives.

If faith is "being sure of what we hope for" (Hebrews 11:1), then if I am ever to have a substantial faith, I must begin with a hope out of which can come something of real substance.

A positive mental attitude is important. A person with a positive outlook is much more ready to accept the possibilities of a firm hope. However, the kind of hope that leads to a rock solid faith is more firm than just a bright attitude and positive thinking.

A naturally optimistic person may actually overlook hope if he relies on the strength of his optimism. Hope is not based on personal temperament. If it were, only the bright, cheery people would go to heaven. The melancholic personalities, who think soberly and deeply about life, would be left behind.

Every personality, temperament, and disposition needs a firm hope. You are not a hopeless person just because you are a serious person.

Things hoped for must have substance if we expect to ever have them. That substance is realized by faith. Even though these things have not been acted upon yet, in hope they are nevertheless substantial. Remember that faith is not hope nor is hope faith. They work together but are not synonymous.

Hope is not a shot in the dark. It is in the realm of possibility according to the abilities, character, and purposes of whatever our hope is placed in. This can be true of both the common hope as well as of that greater hope that we are really considering—a biblical hope based in the ability, character, and purposes of God. This goes beyond the personality of the hoper.

For example, whose hope is more real: the cheerleader yelling and jumping joyfully and enthusiastically or the stern-faced coach watching the same high school football game? Unless the team is sorely outclassed, then my guess would be the coach. He knows the potential of the players and the hours they have spent practicing for strength and effectiveness. True potential substance can come out of his hope.

> **"Hope is not a shot in the dark. It is in the realm of possibility according to the abilities, character, and purposes of whatever our hope is placed in."**

So, is strong hope only a calculated or educated guess? No, not at all, because that would again put the responsibility of hope on the hoper. The one who hopes does have a responsibility, to hope in something of substance.

The King James version of Heb 11:1 says, "now faith is the substance of things hoped for."

Hang on, this may get complicated for a moment or two.

Usually when I think of "substance," my first thought is of that which is made of matter. But the word can also refer to the immaterial, the abstract, the realm of the spirit as well. In the realm of either the material or the immaterial, a "substance" has an "essence," that is, that which when broken down to it's basics is without a mixture of anything else. It is what is left after everything else is separated from it, for example, truth.

Truth has substance, though it is not material. You can't pick it up and hold it in your hand. Truth then has essence; it does exist, though we cannot see it or measure it. When you separate all that is false from it, you have a pure, substantial truth.

Substantial truth also involves reality. Reality consists of those things that are actual, unchangeable, and permanent. In relation to this present world, things can be, as we have said, material, concrete, or may be of an immaterial, abstract essence.

In relation to eternity, there are *ultimate* realities. Ultimate reality comes from the unmixed purity of God, who is spirit, so it is of a primarily spiritual nature. By that I mean only the spiritual nature that would come from God is ultimate reality. That is not to say that matter is not real; it is, but it has come from the creation of God who is spiritually real. He is at His very essence substantially real.

Satan exists in reality but lacks the qualities of the ultimate reality that we find in God. Satan's power and influence are not permanent. He is changeable. Though spiritual in nature, there is an impurity in him that does not produce anything of real substance. For example, he is the Father of Lies. That which he tempts us with is less than substantial; he simply lies about the things of substance. He gives only false hope.

For instance, in the Garden the fruit of the tree was materially real. It had substance in itself because it was created by God. In itself, because it was God's creation, it was good. God had even said it was good. Materially there was real substance, and immaterially as well; behind the fruit was the ultimate reality of God's command. Satan tempted Adam and Eve with twisted truth and lies about the fruit that was real. Do you see the problem? Adam and Eve attempted to put their "faith" in a substance (the fruit) "hoped for" but their hope was misguided by failing to believe the ultimate reality behind the material real.

We must be careful to understand and obey the commands of God. We cannot expect to have a fulfillment of our hope if we have placed our hope in something less than the ultimate reality of God.

The problem I often have is that I hope for a substance that is material but have not hoped for the essence behind it that comes from God. If I put my "hope" on material things, I may misunderstand what God's "substance" is. Our desires often get fixed on earthly substances. We temporarily forget the ultimate reality of God's ability, character, and purposes.

The first question we must ask ourselves if we are to analyze our hope is, Where did this hope come from? Was it birthed in the heart of God? If so, our hope will not compromise God's character, it will not underestimate His ability, nor will it be presumptuous of His purposes.

The kind of hope we need and that God has for us will be distinctly marked by His character which is holy, righteous, and true. God is also good, and in His goodness He displays His love, kindness, mercy, and grace. Therefore, we expect our hope to fall in line with these qualities.

If the slightest hint of impurity is in the hopeful desire you have in your heart, because God is pure in His holiness, then you know the desire can't be from Him. If anything about that desire is not correct, or if the need to justify the desires is beyond its ability to stand unqualified, then seriously question its origin.

Hope that is not in agreement with the fruit of the Spirit is not from God. I must always measure my expectations of God by my ability to hope in a spiritual manner.

Many years ago I had great problems with a particular man. In my estimation he was destroying far more than he was contributing to the good. Our relationship was intolerable. I had a terrible attitude about him. I argued with God that this man was hurting God's own work. I reminded God that this person was giving a bad name to Christianity because he was not a good man. I was secure in my defense of the truth and goodness of God. But in my wish for this man's removal from his position, there was no love for him. My hope for his removal was not from God; in my hope I was compromising God's character, God's fruit in my life. God is love and I had no loving wishes for God's dealing with this man.

We cannot underestimate God's abilities in our hope either. When we are looking for a substantial hope that will lead to a great faith, we must never rule out the miraculous. The supernatural must have a part in our hopes; otherwise we put God on a merely human level.

Do not try to limit the Almighty God in either power or time. Does God ever lay aside His ability to know everything or to be everywhere? Then why would we expect Him to be limited in His power? Because of His unchanging nature, is it not reasonable that miracles are possible? If so, then why should we be afraid to hope in the miraculous?

The subject of the miraculous can be very sensitive. Possibly this is due to the excesses or extremes in opposite directions: denial or presumption. The problem with both extremes is that both have man as a source of hope.

Those who would not trust the miraculous are left to hope only in what man can understand or see or be a part of in the material. Often such people can be very practical, good, solid people, but their hope is limited to the strength of their understanding.

At the other extreme are those who have impertinent expectations in the realm of the miraculous, hoping for something that comes out of their own personal desires. Many times these desires are admirable and certainly understandable, especially in cases where people are believing for healings or miracles for someone else.

Put the extremes aside. Do not base an argument on either. Rather, let us agree that God is a God who is infinitely able. He is able to do the miraculous, able to reveal himself, able to be communicated with, able to drop hope in our hearts for things that go beyond the apparent. From God comes all substance. A hope that has its source in Him is therefore very strong.

A strong hope that comes from the heart of God cannot be presumptuous of the purposes of God.

I'm told that three Bible school students went out one Sunday to preach at an outstation church some distance from school. It had rained most of the night. As their car approached a low spot in the country back road, they saw that a flash flood had made the road impassable.

Feeling the urgency of their task and remembering that God had parted the waters for both Moses and Joshua, they jumped out of the car praying fervently.

Their desire for the miraculous led to action. Moses had a rod, but they didn't. They rolled up a copy of a denominational magazine and struck the waters. All they got was a wet magazine.

To presume is to take upon ourselves the responsibility of knowing. How can I know what the Almighty God wants without asking Him and getting His response? What is His purpose for my life or for any given situation? Either we know the answers, or we don't. If we do, then no problem. If we don't and claim that we do, that's presumption.

There are many things we do know for certain about God, because God has revealed himself to us, His creation. Many aspects of His purposes as well as His promises are abundantly clear because they are written in His Word. The Word of God is substantial. Our hope must be based on what God has revealed clearly to us.

When we venture past the clearly defined aspects of knowing the purposes of God as they are found in His Word, we can have troubles. Some answers are extremely hard to know; some questions have no scriptural references that give crystal-clear direction. Still the answers must be in line with the unalterable principles of the Word of God. A step into the thin air of baseless proclamation is not the answer. However, a proclamation of faith based on the principles and character of God is strong and substantial.

Answers cannot come from within ourselves; they must come from God. We cannot be presumptuous and act on our own wishes. We must find out what God wants. How do we find out? Well, how do you find out the answer to any question? You ask and then wait for an answer. When God answers through His Word, in prayer, or in any other way, hope wells up within us and we are encouraged to follow up in a step of faith.

God, the Creator of all things substantial, has hopes for His people that are real things, and they can be realized through faith. We must grab hold of a hope that has true, potential substance so we won't be disappointed or confused.

A confusing area where we must learn to differentiate is in our desires. Some of our inner longings are from God, some are not. Which is which? Which is a desire of a godly hopeful nature that we should pursue, and which is more of the nature of lust that we should shun?

H. W. Barnett was my pastor for most of my early life. He often spoke about his Bible school days, particularly the day he noticed an especially pretty, young girl on campus. She also noticed him. The students were not allowed to date or hardly even talk to each other, but one day she managed to get a note to him that had a Scripture reference on it: Psalms 37:4— "Delight yourself in the Lord and he will give you the desires of your heart."

In this case, the desires proved to be of God. They married and had a successful life and ministry. Such a hope was biblical, pure, and worthy of action.

"Delight yourself in the Lord and he will give you the desires of your heart."

Our desires need to be examined for biblical worth and purity. What would the end of our desires be if we were able to give them full advantage? Would it be a good result?

One Sabbath day Jesus was in a synagogue where there was a man with a shriveled hand. People, knowing Jesus' reputation because of His miracles and His unorthodox teachings, looked on intently. What would He do this time?

Jesus knew their hearts. He knew the kinds of desires they had. They said things that sounded good, but something else was hidden deep inside. He posed to them a simple but revealing question: "'Which is lawful on the Sabbath: to do good or to do evil, to save life or to kill?'" (Mark 3:4).

Two sets of opposites are given in that short question. The second is an intensifier of the first. A person who would "do good," given the opportunity to follow his heart to its fullest extent, would be involved in things that would "save life." A person who would "do evil," given the chance, would "kill." Such a person has a murderous heart.

Jesus posed a question that clearly showed what hearts they had. They would stop Him from doing good because their hearts were murderous. In fact, some of them left the scene of a miraculous work of God to go out and plot the death of Jesus.

Our desires might seem lofty and noble. We may have great schemes that seem full of good and hope. What does a close examination reveal? What is behind our righteous indignation? What motive lurks behind our desires for an exalted position? Where would that fleeting look lead if given opportunity? If fear of being found out was removed, what compromise of integrity might we make?

If we can survive a heart examination of our desires, then we can identify those that lead to good results. Hope is in those desires. Does God give us what our hearts desire, or does He give us the right kind of heart desires? We should prefer the latter. If we know that our desires are His desires, then they are beyond a fanciful wish; they are of substantial possibilities. Then we can act upon those hopeful desires in faith. It's up to us. At that point God has done His part in giving His desires.

Hope must be substantial. It must be from pure desires and motives. It must come from the heart of God.

CHAPTER SIX

After Loss - Hope

We were at our first church picnic in Bangladesh. It was much different than the ones we had attended in the States. For one thing, it was not as active as picnics I had been to before. I got to try my hand at cricket, which is a very slow-paced game compared to our football or even baseball. My wife, Sharon, and others played Scrabble and other board games that you normally don't think of in connection with an outdoor picnic.

The menu was different too. We had rice and curry, which meant we had to bring the three-foot in diameter pots to cook in, along with hired cooks. The cooks dug a hole and built the fire. They put the big pots over the top. They would boil the rice over one hole, curried chicken over another, and dal over another. Dal is a lentil soup for pouring over the rice. Dal is either yellow or green. The yellow is better than the green.

The picnic spot at the national forest was crowded with people. Most were simply taking strolls in groups through the skinny trees of the forest. Ladies wore saris, and men wore suits or some other outfit better than I was used to seeing for picnic attire. Most of those taking time for picnics would have been of the middle to upper levels of Bangladesh society.

Other people were at the picnic grounds too. All were uninvited. They were obviously poor, and most were children. I saw the cooks pick up sticks and chase several off through the trees, yelling threats all the way. At that point I really didn't understand what was going on except for the obvious fact that the kids were a nuisance to the cooks.

Later the food was ready. We began to eat the spicy Bengali food with our fingers, as is the custom. It's messy, to say the least. Each person plunges his palms into rice with a spicy gravy and squishes it all around to make little rice balls.

While sitting cross-legged on the ground eating with our fingers in Bengali fashion, I noticed the little beggar kids slowly beginning to filter back into the picnic area our church had reserved. At first I didn't think about it. Then I began to feel uneasy and even embarrassed as I sat eating a good Bengali meal while these little Bengali beggars watched.

Someone near me finished his meal and put the tin platter down as he went to wash his hands. One of the children rushed over to scoop the scraps into the little bag he carried. As others finished, the process was repeated over and over again with fierce competition among the kids for our picnic scraps.

"Hope is made of that which has attached itself to our hearts. Real hope cannot be taken from us."

I sat shocked and saddened, not knowing how to deal with my emotions. I have never known a time of such want or hunger in my own life. I don't know even now, after seeing gross poverty daily for years, what it is like to personally be in such a state of want. God has blessed us.

Yet after years of seeing such scenes (and worse), I am still amazed that beggar children play and act as if living on the streets is normal. For them, it is.

How can people with nothing have hope?

Hope is not in possessions. Hope of any form is buried inside the person and is of no material worth. Hope is made of that which has attached itself to our hearts. Real hope cannot be taken from us.

Much of the strength of hope is a result of overcoming the sense of loss. When there is nothing to lose, then there is no sense of loss. That's why at times people who have nothing to begin with seem to recover more readily than others in time of devastation. They have not attached their hopes to things of much earthly value anyway.

One of the most amazing things about Job was his position in the face of devastating losses. Everything he could possibly call his had been taken away, except his own life and his hope in God. Still his hope was so strong he said even if God would slay him he would still hope in Him.

We must be careful of where we place our hope. Is our hope in something that can be taken away? If it is, when that thing is taken, our hope goes with it. If we put an inordinate amount of hope on anything or any person, the loss of that possession or the death or removal of that person can destroy our hope. If we cannot overcome loss, we will lose hope. If we lose hope, all that is left is despair. Despair leads only to destruction in some form.

Victor Frankl is known for his writings that came from his experiences in Nazi concentration camps during World War II. He was a witness and a victim of the depravation and cruelty that can strip a person of every earthly possession but his soul. He remembered the men who walked through the huts giving away their last piece of bread. They demonstrated that everything can be taken but one thing: the freedom to choose their attitude.

The real battles to be fought are inside of us. Loss or gain are perceptions that can be more important to our mental and spiritual well-being than the reality. The perception that all hope is gone is usually devastating. Chuck Swindoll calls attention to the "Broken Heart" study cited by Douglas Colligan in *New York* magazine. The study researched the death rate of 4,500 widowers within six months of their wives' deaths. It found that the widowers were 40 percent more likely to die than other men of the same age.

Hope is entirely future oriented. To reach the place where there is no possibility of the future brings the inward devastation. If there is no hopeful eternity nor any hopeful earthly future, what can possibly be left? If a person has convinced himself that nothing of value is in the future, then despair and devastation are inevitable.

Frankl helps us see this idea from his experiences and observations. Prisoners who had lost faith in the future were doomed. Losing a belief in the future caused them to decline mentally, physically, and spiritually. It usually began with a prisoner refusing to get up in the morning. He simply gave up.

Frankl also saw through one prisoner the link between the loss of faith in the future and giving up. The prisoner told him of his dream that liberation would come to the camp March 30, 1945.

The man was full of hope and convinced that his dream would be right. As March 30 drew nearer, the war news made it appear very unlikely that the prisoners would be free. On March 29 the man suddenly ran a high temperature. On March 30 he became delirious and lost consciousness. On March 31 he was dead. To all outward appearances, he had died of typhus.

Frankl attributes the ultimate cause of the man's death to severe disappointment, which suddenly lowered his body's resistance against the latent typhus infection. "His faith in the future and his will to live had become paralyzed and his body fell victim to illness. Thus the voice of his dream was right after all."

Most things only appear hopeless. No one can take away our hope; it can only be surrendered. When it is surrendered, we have lost sight of everything, including God. Only then is there no hope. One of the most precious things we have to guard is our hope. Therefore, our hope must be anchored in something very strong. What we place our hope in must be invincible; it cannot be placed in people or in possessions. Both can be taken or destroyed.

The illustration that Jesus used, mentioning how hard it is for the rich to enter the Kingdom, focuses on the difficulty people of means have with loss. The "eye of the needle" is difficult for the camel to go through (whether it is understood as the hole in a sewing needle or as a small opening in the wall where a camel had to be unloaded in order to crawl through). The point is that people of means find it hard to suffer earthly loss because their hope is in what was lost.

In contrast to those who hold on too tightly to things that can be taken away, the apostle Paul says:

I consider everything a loss compared to the surpassing greatness of knowing Christ Jesus my Lord, for whose sake I have lost all things.

I consider them rubbish, that I may gain Christ and be found in him (Philippians 3:8-9).

Paul is not complaining and taking a "poor me" posture. He is emphasizing the priority of his life, which is Christ who cannot be taken away from him. In comparison to Christ, everything else of earthly value is junk.

Whether the losses we sustain are possessions, loved ones, position, or anything on which we place great value, we must guard our ultimate hope in the surety of God's promises.

Please be careful if you are in a time of loss, whether it is the loss of property due to some natural calamity, or the loss of a child, or a divorce, or a great opportunity or position that has fallen through. Hold on to hope. Look beyond the crisis or disappointment. Talk to someone you know will listen. Don't dwell on the problem. Take a step back and rest if needed. Change activities for a while to get a better perspective of things that matter. Do whatever you need to do to see beyond the darkness of the thing that looks as though it is robbing the very existence of your future.

Cancer is not the end, neither is AIDS nor leukemia. God has a future for all who trust in Him. We have hope even in our times of loss.

CHAPTER SEVEN

In the Face of "Slow and Constant Erosion"

It's the slow and constant erosion of your soul." I don't know how many times I heard Howard Hawkes say that phrase in the few years we had together in Bangladesh. He was ending a long, solid missionary career of thirty-five years, and I was on a shaky start.

At first I thought, *This poor old guy sure is negative.* But something didn't fit with my evaluation. Howard was mostly a positive kind of man. He used his little phrase when something hadn't gone well, when there was a misunderstanding with someone, or when any one of a million other unfortunate incidents had happened. The glint in his eye and the chuckle in his voice revealed he was merely commenting on tough situations that would rob my joy if I couldn't develop that same attitude.

Much of what happened in our first two years on the field I can laugh at now. It was certainly one of those periods of "the slow and constant erosion of our souls." My ability to maintain a hopeful attitude was daily being challenged beyond what I thought I was able to bear.

Bangladesh offers every opportunity for one's soul to be eroded into hopelessness if allowed. *Erosion* is the perfect word. Things just seem to happen in Bangladesh. It seems they continue to happen without end. One day you realize many of the difficult things will never change significantly for the better; in fact, they may get worse. Sounds terribly pessimistic, but that's the way it can seem when you have come believing in your heart that you may be in this new land until you die. After a few months, when first experiences have become commonplace and the problems mount incessantly, you face days when you wonder how you will ever make it for the long haul. You can. You will. It just seems impossible at times.

Bangladesh is one of the poorest, most overpopulated, disaster-prone countries of the world. For a population of over 150 million people, plus an annual increase of over 3 million—in an area the size of Arkansas—things don't look too bright for the future.

I remember the first time I heard the term *third world*. I had to search to find it meant the "developing countries." At the time I had the understanding that it meant the "poorer countries." Now some are beginning to talk about a "fourth world," which are nations where little economic hope for the future exists. Such people suggest that in these fourth world countries aid should be withdrawn and used more profitably in other places. In other words, just give up on these fourth world countries. Bangladesh has been mentioned as one of those countries.

When we first came to Bangladesh, I was like most missionaries: full of hope to change things, to do great things for God, and to turn the tide toward the gospel. I don't think I am much different now, except for a better understanding of the obstacles.

Obstacles are opportunities to either develop or destroy hope. We get to choose which it will be. The circumstances do not dictate our response; therefore, the choice is ours to make. Never choose anything less than that which is hopeful. Little is as helpful as that which is hopeful.

Our first two years on the field were trying times. Nothing seemed hopeful then. We have had tougher times since those beginning days, but those two years were unique for us; all was so new and so different and so challenging. I can laugh about most of it now, but it wasn't easy to laugh then.

The conditions of the country itself were very undeveloped. At times during the days of adjustment, the reality of the situation was overwhelming. In those times I realized I had made a conscious decision to move my wife, my family, and my future to one of the most difficult areas of the world to live. I had no one to blame. I felt God had directed me and then I did everything I could to go to Bangladesh. Many days I had to remind myself that I had begged the mission leaders of my denomination to let me come.

"Obstacles are opportunities to either develop or destroy hope. We get to choose which it will be."

The church we had come to work with was extremely small. In the whole country less than a third of a percent even call themselves Christian, and many of them are merely nominal Christians. Our group nationwide could not have numbered two thousand, and there were major divisions within that small handful. We had only about a dozen churches even though the work had started in the 1940s. We still didn't have one church that was supporting its pastor. We did have missionaries. In fact, we had more missionaries than national workers!

I wanted to start things off in a good way, especially with my colleagues. I didn't. Things got worse. In the papers of another country that I visited, I was accused of being a CIA agent. That news was picked up by Moscow Radio and beamed throughout the region using my name. I was blacklisted in that country. To make matters more ominous, I was called to the U.S. Embassy to explain myself. I still think some of our own people were not sure if I was a spy or not.

Then I accidentally broke a senior missionary lady's arm. It was an innocent accident, but it required special attention, sapping time and energy of fellow workers.

Besides that, we had problems at home—not marital problems, nor problems with our children. We had servant problems. It sounds great to have servants to run errands and do the work. Wrong. Rather than an employer-employee type of relationship, it was more like adding grown adults to our family. In most cases the servants live with the employer. Sure, they are a help—after a while. At first they had demands and needs. They couldn't speak our language. We misunderstood them, and they misunderstood us. But we needed help to set up a household, and we needed someone to watch the kids while we went to language school. We also needed someone who could go to the male-dominated open market where some of the younger fellows liked to take the raw meat and put it in front of my wife's face. We also needed a guard or someone might steal from us. In short, having household help can be a headache even if all goes well.

Things didn't go well. In that two-year period we were robbed twice by servants. We hired and fired two "ayahs," the ladies who baby-sat our children during language school. We had four different houseboys, six cooks, and seven chokidars (guards). They were not highly paid, and we didn't have more than three working at any one time, which are three more than we really wanted.

Add in the frustrations of not being able to communicate, dealing with a totally new culture, bearing extreme heat and humidity, waiting for mail that took a minimum of a month's turnaround time, and not being able to make a phone call because even after four years' worth of applications, we still couldn't get a phone.

Also remember the days when we'd just lathered shampoo in our hair in the shower only to have the water go off for the day, or to have supper cooking on the electric cooker only to have the electricity out until the afternoon.

To that setting, add even more problems. We had seven automobile accidents. I was hit by a bus, a car, two rickshas, and two bicycles. A man carrying a thirty-foot bamboo on his head hit the car with the end of the bamboo and sheared the molding off the car. All of them happened while I was sitting still in the car!

We had a new car, yet after a few months I spent more time push-starting it than starting it with a key. Almost every morning our whole family could be seen running down the road trying to push-start our bright lime-green car. Then one night someone put sand in my tank.

That clogged up things for a while. I had twenty-four flat tires in those two years, sometimes two at a time.

Other things happened too. Eight times Sharon discovered by sense of smell where rats had climbed into the back of the electric stove and were electrocuted. Rats got into the clothes closet when we were out of the city and shredded the hems of most of Sharon's dresses.

We also had electrical problems. The better houses are made of cement and brick. The older ones then have the water pipes and electric wiring visible on the outside of the walls. Our landlord had been overseas often and got the idea that it would be best to hide the unsightly pipes and wires. It did look much better, but the electric wires burned someplace inside the walls. The problem then was to find out where, because the burned wires became impossible to pull through the conduit. The cement and brick had to be chiseled out until the problem was located. That meant having a crew of four or five men tearing up our walls and then repairing them. The process took four or five days each time. It happened five times in those first two years!

Bad news came from the States for us too. One letter came from my mother saying a storm had torn off part of the roof of our house. The repair nearly depleted our savings. Later a telegram came with this disturbing news: "Dad fell, two legs broken, pray." For two weeks we had no idea what had happened. Then we found out he had twenty-seven broken places, requiring surgery and eighteen metal pins.

We were still in our first year when a fellow missionary named Ken rushed in to where the rest of us were celebrating the Fourth of July. He had his passport in hand and a startled, agitated look on his face that said something hadn't gone well.

Ken had been given ten days to leave the country. The eviction notice was not just for him; it was for all of us. Our appeals were finally accepted, but we had many anxious weeks of not knowing if we would be able to stay to minister in the place we had waited years to reach.

I wish I could say things got better in time. They didn't. Pressures of various sorts constantly arose through the many years since, often more intense and challenging than those beginning experiences. In those first two years, I learned that when I challenged the way things were and planned for progress, I'd have problems. Problems are inevitable.

The question we must deal with is how will we face our problems? We can face them in fear and doubt, and they will chase us away. Or we can face them in hope and faith and conquer them one day at a time. Howard wasn't being negative with his erosion comment. Life will, day by day, eventually erode our strength and health. That is inevitable because we are mortal. The trick is to learn the little chuckle that says hope has taken hold of your attitude. Little is as attractive to anyone as a person who has gone through great problems and is still full of bright hope. Hope is contagious.

"The question we must deal with is how will we face our problems?"

The Lord does let us go through times that stretch us beyond former limits. Recognize that hope is in those challenges. We have hope that we will be able to conquer problems we have never conquered before, while learning new insights and adding strength for future challenges.

We also hope that, just as we made it through yesterday's grief or obstacle, anything facing us today will in the same way be put behind us. Tomorrow it will be only a memory. We choose whether we will smile about the obstacle or let the bitterness of it sap our hopeful walk toward faith. Step by step, in the toughest of times, we must faithfully continue holding onto every glimmer of hope; this hope will keep us over the long haul.

CHAPTER EIGHT

Bigger than Our Crises

The day after Christmas 1982, I left for Lebubari in the marshland area of Bangladesh. We were going for youth meetings that were to last four days. It would also take two days to get there and two days to get back.

Lebubari is typical of Bangladesh's sixty-nine thousand villages. There is no electricity in the bamboo houses. Almost always small ponds or canals are nearby to bathe in. Coconut and various other trees offer shade from the sun. Villages aren't what I would have expected prior to coming to Bangladesh; most villages are just a few huts with a few families scattered in a given area. Hardly anything distinguishes one cluster of huts from another.

The place where we stayed was in a remote area of the country on a piece of land built up above the fields. During some months the fields are under more than ten feet of water, leaving the house and small land around it like a little island. From the few visible distant huts a group of about one hundred young people came to the youth meetings we were holding.

Steve Alexander had come with me. We were staying in the attic area of a fairly well made tin-covered house. Most houses are one-roomed bamboo huts. This one, by village standards, was very nice. It had several rooms plus the small attic area. In the attic, mats were stretched over the boards and we put our covers on top. We climbed a ladder to our temporary quarters.

At 7:00 Wednesday morning, December 30, 1982, the last day of our Lebubari youth meetings, I woke up to see Steve climb to the top of the ladder. From the look on his face I knew something was wrong.

Then I learned the news. A phone call had reached a subdivisional town several miles away the day before. From there a couple of men were sent to bring the message to me. Anxiously I waited as Steve told me the message they brought was not at all good. My three-year-old son had fallen and hurt his head.

These men had traveled all night just to tell me that Luke had hurt his head. That was all they knew. They had no details. I was confused. I had hardly enough information to be alarmed, yet something wasn't right. At that point, I didn't know if I should start back or finish with our plans.

A few minutes later, as we were outside talking with the messengers, we saw another man coming across the fields toward us. When I was finally able to recognize the man, I knew the accident was serious. The man approaching us worked at the Dhaka Center. I knew he would be coming only to bring a message. I also knew it took two days for him to get to where we were.

The man told me Luke had indeed fallen and hurt his head. Blood was coming out of his ear. He also said I should get back to Dhaka as soon as possible.

I was ready to go right away, but everyone told me I couldn't leave then. At first I couldn't understand why. Then they explained that the river current was going the wrong way. Travel would be too slow. Besides that, the launch I would need to catch would not be there until later. They suggested it would be best to finish the last morning youth meeting. Then when the tide changed, we could go more easily and still have more than enough time to reach the launch on time.

It seemed an eternity until at last we could go. I left Steve and the youth group and traveled the next four or five hours toward the small town where the launch to Dhaka would stop.

I stood and waited, looking in the general direction from which the launch should come. I waited hour after endless hour there. No launch.

To those who were also waiting for the launch and to the hawkers and the children who were constantly at the docks, I was an oddity. Not many foreigners would make their way to back areas where that particular dock is located.

Normally in that situation I would have had fun with the curious crowd. That day was not a normal day. Someplace in Dhaka my son was injured, and I didn't know if he was alive or dead. If he had been dead I might not have ever been able to see him on this earth again. In Bangladesh if a person dies, he is usually buried the same day. Because of my impatient, disturbed frame of mind the onlookers were beginning to get on my nerves.

The sunset was probably beautiful, but I don't recall anything of beauty that day. Only the orange-red glow on the clouds overhead remained when the launch lights first appeared. Fortunately, it was one of the larger launches on its way down this fork of the Ganges River, which empties into the Bay of Bengal.

The launch was six hours late.

A ten- or twelve-inch wide plank was lowered from the launch to the ground as the scramble began. First, those who were departing the launch balanced on their heads the burlap bags of goods they were transporting either to or from the market. They cautiously made their way down the plank. One slight misstep could cause them to drop the bags that, in some cases, took two men to lift to their heads.

Then, for us on the ground came the mayhem of pushing and jostling into position with our baggage or whatever goods our group had to carry up the plank. Most were concerned about getting a good position on the open deck where the bracing night air would blow through their thin clothing if they didn't get a protected spot.

Debu, the messenger who had been sent from Dhaka, was with me. I sent him to find out if we could possibly get a "first-class" arrangement. To my surprise, with the crowd that was already on the launch, we were able to get a small cabin. The cabin was only about five- by six-feet with two benches on opposite walls, but it was ours for the night. Debu soon went to sleep. I didn't.

It seems as if Bangladesh is never quiet. That is especially true of the town areas. Even the villages, as peaceful as they seem to be, are often full of sound. The "noise" of unanswered questions inside me was much more disturbing.

I know the greatest battleground in spiritual warfare is in the mind. I wish I had a solution that would allow a person to always win those battles. We can win most of those battles, but I am realistic enough to know that even the most committed saint from time to time falls into temporary depression or to some other trick of the enemy. We must not fall into the succeeding trap: self-condemnation.

"Have you ever questioned God? It is not wrong to question God, as long as you are looking for answers from God."

I wish I could say I spent that night in deep faith-building prayer. I did not. I spent the night worrying. As I sat in that tiny dark cabin infested with cockroaches and listened to the constant disturbances and voices, my mind reeled off unpleasant pictures.

I recalled every struggle of the past two years-the constant battles that daily erode the soul and strength and pick away at patience and resolve. Maybe there was something wrong with me. Maybe I had missed God. Maybe I hadn't really heard His voice. Maybe my imagination had gotten the best of me.

Have you ever questioned God? It is not wrong to question God, as long as you are looking for answers from God. That's not the kind of questioning I was doing that night. I was allowing depressing thoughts and questions to take hold.

God are you really there? I hadn't had those doubts since I had accepted Christ as Savior. *God, if you are there, why is there even such a place as Bangladesh?* Probably more heaped-up heartbreak is in this little land on a consistent basis than on any other piece of real estate in the world. Would a loving, caring God allow a Bangladesh? One out of four or five children do not survive birth. The next 25 percent won't live to see their fifth birthday. Would a God of love allow such constant suffering?

I continued to question. *God, why has there never been a significant move of acceptance of the gospel by many in this land? Don't you care that over 150 million souls are probably doomed to an eternity without even hearing an adequate witness of the gospel? Can't you grant a special visitation that would stop the hands of your adversaries? Can't you allow greater power to your people? If you are omnipotent, then why don't you do something?*

Then I got to the issue at hand that was really bothering me. It was a test of my faith in a loving, Heavenly Father. *We suffer attacks from the devil on a consistent basis. Don't you love Bangladesh? Don't you love me? Why did you allow this accident to happen? Why my son? Have I sinned? Am I out of your will? Did you really bring me here? Are you there, God?*

I wasn't looking for answers. I was venting my anger at God, while in my heart I was making plans to quit. The pressure of the past two years, capped off by this latest disaster, was taking its toll. If we can be tempted to give in to despair and give up hope, our faith will crumble. Then sooner or later, we will crumble too.

Despair is the absence of hope. With the absence of hope there can be no faith. We must not allow ourselves to be sucked into a spiral of wrong responses to difficult situations. We must hold on to hope. Our faith may falter. Those are ugly times when it does, but faith can recover as long as there is a valid hope. We must not let hope be extinguished; if it is, despair is its replacement.

Twenty-six hours after I had started my trip, I got off the rickshaw in front of our home. As I opened the gate, I saw my wife Sharon coming out of the house. She was just getting ready to go back to the hospital where she had spent the last four days and three nights with Luke. The accident had happened Monday morning; it was now Thursday afternoon.

She began to cry as she told me that Luke was alive, though in serious condition. We got into the car and started toward the hospital.

On the way she told me what had happened.

We had built a small bamboo hut playhouse for the children for a Christmas present. It was built on stilts to discourage rats and other creatures from taking up residence. It was only two and a half feet off the ground, but the steps led to the cement driveway. Luke had fallen from the top of the steps and landed on his head.

After one doctor x-rayed Luke, he said Luke probably had a fractured skull. Sharon took Luke to find the office of a neurosurgeon who had been recommended. He confirmed that it was a fractured skull. He said the hospital would not be a good place for Luke because of the unsanitary conditions, but because of the nature of the injury and the possibility of hemorrhage, it would be best that he be in the hospital in case immediate surgery would become necessary.

Luke was taken immediately to one of the best hospitals in the whole country. Nothing was available except a ward bed. Sharon took it. Together she and Luke climbed to the fifth floor to settle in for the first night.

The children's ward was filled with children and their mothers, and friends, relatives, servants, and hospital personnel. No partitions provided privacy. Mothers or a female representative had to stay with the child through the night because no one else was there to watch the children. Sharon would have to spend the night sharing a small twin-size bed with three-year-old Luke. The prospects of rest were slim. The first night Sharon had no idea she would have several more days of the same.

On Tuesday blood was still coming out of Luke's ear. That meant at least another day and night in the hospital. On Wednesday the blood had turned into a clear liquid. A young intern had told Sharon it was a good sign. Sharon began telling Luke they were going to get to go home. She was as ready to leave as Luke was. She'd had to stay with him night and day, except for the few times someone would stay with Luke giving her a short break.

Later a group of the young people came by the hospital to visit. Among them was a young Malaysian man named Bernard who was in Bangladesh studying medicine. Sharon began to tell him that since the clear liquid had started to flow, it looked as though they would be able to go home soon. As she spoke, the expression on Bernard's face changed. He took the youth leader aside and the two went to find the doctor.

Bernard had understood that instead of good news, the spinal fluid that surrounds the brain had begun to drain, which was a serious sign. Complications could set in, including the possibility of contracting meningitis. We had no way to know what was really happening or what might happen still. Sharon's hopes had sunk to a new low.

My twenty-six hours of travel without knowing what was ahead had been miserable, but Sharon's four days of caring for our son had been worse.

We arrived at the hospital. I wish I could say I walked into that ward with faith, hope, and cheer radiating from me. After all, I'm a missionary. I'm supposed to be a man of God; I was sent by God as a man of faith, not as a man of failure and defeat. I wish I could say my faith and trust were unmoved. I can't. I was near despair.

I was scared, even afraid to see my own son. I didn't know what he would look like. I had never had to deal with such a serious situation in my immediate family. I feared it would be life-altering. I didn't know if I would be able to cope.

As I came to the area of the ward where Luke was, I noticed familiar faces of friends. Then at about the same time that I saw Luke, he saw me. To my total relief, he smiled.

I don't know exactly when, but I know that sometime in that miserable place, God touched my little boy.

That day the fluid stopped draining and blood started again. By the next day the blood had stopped flowing. Saturday morning Luke came home.

I relearned a great lesson. God loves us in spite of our doubts, in spite of our fears, and in spite of our failure to perform acts of faith in the midst of a crisis.

Faith on my part is small, like a mustard seed. We had been blindsided by a crisis. My faith had no courageous pronouncements. Even through very serious questioning my faith was simply the trusting kind that knows God really is there. It may have been the faith of others that was honored for Luke's healing. I don't know. I only know God loves me if I have great faith or little faith. He really doesn't have to prove anything to me. He does not require that I prove myself to Him either, except through my simple trust that He is my God, and I belong to Him.

> ## "God loves us in spite of our doubts, in spite of our fears, and in spite of our failure to perform acts of faith in the midst of a crisis."

All I had through the crisis was a glimmer of hope. Such personal crises are a definite challenge to faith and hope. Hope helps us hold on in such times of weakness and confusion when it seems very difficult to be strong in an active faith.

I can't answer why God would spare my son and yet others would lose theirs. He could have just as easily allowed him to be taken. I was not more worthy than they.

I don't believe it was an exercise of my faith that allowed Luke to live and be healed, even though that was the thing that pleased me most. I do believe it was a great God who loves and who knows what is best. With this attitude I could be accused of being fatalistic, but in fatalism blind chance determines the outcome. I, however, have faith in a God who gives us hope for the best.

I've been with those who have lost love ones. They usually have the same question: Why? I have no answer except for my deep belief that God knows why, and someday He will tell us. God is bigger than my doubts. In Him there is hope that, in spite of it all, things will still work out for good, even when it looks the opposite.

If you would ask me to sacrifice my son, Luke, for you or for anyone in this world, I would absolutely refuse. No one would be that important. If the giving of his young life would save even a hundred others, I know I could not bring myself to willingly allow it. That's the love I now know a father has for his own child. God loved us enough that He gave His only Son Jesus for you and me. Why? I have no complete answer to that kind of love, only gratitude.

What problem do we have that is so great it exceeds Christ's sacrifice on the cross? The cross seems like a big crisis. Yet it is the very wisdom of God. Why should we be tempted to think that a lesser problem of ours would be too big for God? It only appears to be too big when we have temporarily lost sight of hope.

Why should we believe faith is a tool to get us out of all the hurt that life's crises may bring when God would not use faith as a tool to escape His own pain? Suffering was a part of God's plan for Jesus. Would it be wrong for suffering to be a part of God's plan for us?

I have problems. Quite possibly your problems are many times more complex or heartrending than mine. Still, neither of us is hanging naked on a tree, dying innocently for someone else's sin. Jesus died for our sin. We deserved the cross; Jesus didn't.

Our crisis is not as eternally important as that which Christ faced for us. That is the point: Our crisis is not too big for Jesus. Christ conquered the ultimate crisis for us. Can He not also be in control of our problem and do that which is best? Hope is available for us even in the time of crisis and in spite of our doubts.

.

CHAPTER NINE

Assassins of Hope

Hope is not easy to maintain in a world such as ours. Too many assassins of hope are lying in wait. We must do our best to avoid these assassins. Let me caution you about a few of them.

One assassin of hope is a wrong view of our circumstances. None of us had the luxury of choosing our parents. I love my parents, but they didn't let me vote on a very important decision—my birth! I had nothing to say about where or when I was born, what our family income would be, or what kind of house we would live in. I had little to do with how they treated me, except for a few situations that I provoked. I had no choice about nationality, skin color, and genetic makeup. I would have made other choices had I been given the chance. I would like to be six-foot-two, but I'm stuck with five-foot-nine.

Our biblical hope is not based in this world's advantages or disadvantages. If it were, we could complain against God justly. Jesus never promised us a just world; therefore, a cry for justice in the world is somewhat irrelevant. God is a just God, but this world isn't just. Since it isn't, then what did God promise? Since He is a God of justice, there is an inherent promise that on a personal level He will deal justly with us. He has also promised abundant and eternal life. Our hope is in such promises. In relation to God's abundance we have the promise that He will be fair. Circumstances may seem otherwise, but remember that the awards ceremony is later. Because awards are later, hope and faith are all the more important and the issues of this world are all the less significant.

When reviewing the bigger picture of God's plans, no one can point to God and say He has been unfair. To do so would be to ignore Jesus. "God so loved the world that he gave his one and only Son" (John 3:16). Can we expect more from God than what God has done for His Son?

Let us keep in mind that the greatest of God's abundance is showered upon the "one and only Son." With that in focus consider God's earthly and eternal abundance showered upon Christ.

No one can point to Jesus and say He doesn't understand the dealings of a loving Heavenly Father. In the Gospels Jesus constantly makes the point that He and the Father are one. Yet look how the God-Man Jesus came to the earth and was treated on the basis of being God's one and only Son. The Father did not give Jesus special treatment; He received ordinary treatment, such treatment would be common to us all. Jesus suffered a strong sampling of all the difficulties of humanity.

Jesus was born of questionable birth; His mother was pregnant out of wedlock. He was born in a barn. His parents were not rich. He was born of a race that has been possibly one of the most hated of all time. His nation was subjugated to a power that viewed His country as backward and inferior. Jesus owned nothing but the clothes on His back, and even those were taken from Him.

Jesus was misunderstood by the very people He had come to save. His activities and teachings were under constant scrutiny and criticism. He suffered an unjust trial, was charged with blasphemy in the religious court, and convicted of treason in the civil court. False witnesses testified against Him. One of His closest followers turned Him over to the proceedings that would decide His conviction, another denied ever knowing Him, and most of the others abandoned Him in this critical hour. He then suffered one of the most cruel deaths a person could suffer.

No one can point to Jesus and say He doesn't understand our circumstances. If we have suffered, He has suffered more. Our circumstances do not compare to His. When we see that God allowed the Second Person of the Godhead to become human, suffer, then conquer death and the grave, we can have hope in our circumstances. Isn't our situation better than His was? Jesus didn't come to earth and suffer all those things to show off His superiority; He came to show us that even amid the worst of the world's settings there is hope. He conquered death and the grave and then promised us abundant and eternal life. In our less extenuating circumstances is the hope that we will also make it through triumphantly.

Those who have few tests cannot know the exhilaration and joy of conquering the tough ones.

Our outward situations may rise or fall at the whim of unjust people, at the unexpectedness of natural calamity, or at an unexpected inheritance or great success. No matter what the situation, our hope need never change because it is not based on circumstances. I look toward Jesus as my hope. If my fortune rises or falls, it doesn't matter— because all earthly circumstances are temporary. Good or bad, they all are doomed to history. Hope, however, is always looking past the present conditions to Jesus, who is always our future. Circumstances must not dictate our hope.

Fear is another inward murderer of hope.

Joshua and Caleb understood the promise of God. They were ready to take steps of faith to possess the promise. Others weren't. These two alone kept alive in their hearts hope of what God would do because He had promised. Caleb stood with Joshua as they were ready to part ways after entering the land of God's promise to them. Both were now over eighty years old. Caleb reminisced of how Moses had promised him as his inheritance the hill country where he had been as a spy. His hope had not yet been realized as he asked Joshua to allow him to take the land.

Though Caleb had kept hope alive during those forty years of dismal delay, he recounted with Joshua how his "brothers who went up with [him] made the hearts of the people melt with fear" (Joshua 14:8). That is quite a contrast. Two men full of hope in a promise and ready for faithful action stood and listened as the others who had seen similar things shared an entirely different assessment of the situation. The eight had seen a challenge, and they feared. Their description was saturated with fear-producing pictures. The description of strong giants in big cities with walls to the sky did not give them giant faith; it gave them grasshopper fear. Caleb said their evaluation caused the hearts of the people to melt.

Melting hearts spell fear.

During my first year at Bible school, one of the seniors spoke in a morning chapel meeting. The years have erased his name from my memory, but I remember clearly one illustration in his sermon. He told about how when he was a small child he loved to play with his plastic soldiers in the sandbox. One day his uncle came to visit and brought him a gift. It was a chocolate soldier wrapped in aluminum foil.

He took his new brightly dressed soldier to the sandpile battlefield. Because this soldier was bigger than all the plastic ones, naturally he would be the commander. Pretend battles raged for the rest of the morning as the courageous commander of the forces led the army of choice to victory after victory. Then lunchtime came. There was a reluctant cease-fire as the boy ran to the house, leaving his proud soldier standing in front of the forces.

To his dismay when he returned to the sandbox of battle, he discovered that the heat of the noonday sun had taken its toll. The once valiant-looking chocolate soldier had melted into the sand.

Fear is like that. It stops us in our tracks. The heat of the situation tests the strength of what we are made of. Often what is found is left in a melted, useless lump.

Have you ever noticed how many "fear nots" are recorded in the Bible? Again and again we are told not to fear. Fear is common—too common.

The Bible tells us that "God hath given us the spirit of fear" (2 Timothy 1:7, KJV). If God hasn't given us fear, then it must come from another source. Fear is not what God wants for us, so why do we choose to fear rather than to have faith? Why do we allow ourselves to have a fearful nature rather than a hopeful one?

Hope looks beyond fear. In hope we understand that fear is, more often than not, a façade we have created around a potential problem. There are other ways to face a problem than dwelling on the potential disaster. In any situation we must give hope a hearing. We must consider ways to get over, around, or through the problem facing us.

Fear says "maybe we can't"; hope says "maybe we can." God is a God of hopeful possibilities, not fearful impossibilities. God can. With His help so much more can be done. Hope sees possibilities; fear denies them.

Another deadly attacker of hope is doubt. As an assassin, doubt aims at faith. But hope is also in doubt's sight. And if you kill hope, faith cannot live long. Technically doubt does not seek to destroy either hope or faith; it sets them aside, which has the same detrimental results.

"God is a God of hopeful possibilities, not fearful impossibilities."

Doubt is fear-based. It is the fear of commitment to either belief or unbelief. Jesus constantly dealt with these two great issues of the New Testament—belief and unbelief. Doubt is neither.

Though there is no denial of faith when there is doubt, neither is there acceptance of faith. Doubt hangs in the middle somewhere. While doubt seems to be neutral and not particularly dangerous, it is, in fact, very deceitful and extremely dangerous. What did Jesus say about this lukewarm, middle-of-the-road condition? He said to the Laodicean church, "I know your deeds, that you are neither cold nor hot. I wish you were either one or the other! So, because you are lukewarm—neither hot nor cold—I am about to spit you out of my mouth" (Revelation 3:15-16). In Jesus' mind noncommitment to belief is unbelief.

Doubt is possibly closer to belief than open denial of faith, but as the old saying goes, "*Close* counts only in a game of horseshoes."

It could be argued that hope also stands somewhat in the middle as well. It isn't faith and neither is it truly committed. But hope is the antithesis of doubt. The difference seems to be that hope faces faith, and doubt faces unbelief. No matter how near you are to belief, once you entertain doubt, you begin to turn away from faith. In the same way, no matter how near you may seem to unbelief, when you catch a glimpse of hope, you begin to turn away from unbelief.

Hope directs us Godward; doubt directs us either manward or inward. The direction toward doubt is very dangerous because absolute answers do not come from man nor from inside ourselves. We are not complete enough. Looking solely to a human direction as the source of answers leads only to confusion. Trying to find complete answers from within ourselves only increases doubt because of the compound of confusion. According to Os Guinness, this is "the 'centipede complex,'" based on this nineteenth-century poem:

> The Centipede was happy quite,
> Until the toad in fun,
> Said, "Pray, which leg goes after which?"
> Which worked her mind to such a pitch,
> She lay distracted in a ditch,
> Considering how to run.

Does that mean there is no good in us at all? No, it means we need help. We need to turn our doubt to hope by looking to a more hopeful source than ourselves. That source is "Christ in you, the hope of glory" (Colossians 1:27).

Doubt also questions ability. It questions the ability of God and it questions our own ability. How many times have you begun to question yourself when faced with an opportunity to be a part of a worthwhile project, to enter a race, or to take part in any other venture of great promise or challenge of personal accomplishment?

I blame my doubts for many missed opportunities. In retrospect I should have been a good little league short-stop. I could field fairly well, I was quick, and I was good at getting on base. But I allowed my doubts to keep me from trying.

The first year, fear of failure kept me from trying out at all. The next year I made it to the tryouts and performed well. Then I found out being in the league would mean buying a uniform and paying a five dollar fee. I doubted I would be able to raise the money and I doubted my parents would help me. I didn't even ask. Because of those doubts, which were not even true, all I have now is regret.

We can name dozens of personal examples where doubt has been a traitor of hope, a thief of dreams. We must leave those things in the past and go on. However, let us be historians of our own past. If a thief had stolen from us because the door was open, we would put a lock on the door. Let us lock out doubt, the thief of hope.

Theodore Roosevelt said, "Far better it is to dare mighty things, to win glorious triumphs, even though checkered by failure, than to take rank with those poor spirits who neither enjoy much nor suffer much because they live in the gray twilight that knows neither victory nor defeat."

Self-examination often reveals my weaknesses and faults. Close scrutiny of others often produces the same result. Both bring doubt that hinders rather than helps. Hope finds the strengths and potential in ourselves and others.

Motivational writers and speakers all condemn doubt. Secular motivational personalities push the strengths of a positive person over a negative one. It seems true that a person of confidence, trusting in his abilities without doubt in himself, can accomplish much more than the one filled with doubt. What happens when our strength comes to the end of its ability?

Hope in our abilities is limited; hope in God isn't. I may doubt my own ability and be less accomplished. That in itself is a shame, but it isn't the end of the world. If doubt in God is chosen over hope in Him, however, then faith can never come. That is eternally tragic. Let us entertain hope and defy doubt. Through hope let us find the potential that God sees in us and in others.

Criticism is another sharpshooter that can kill hope.

Nothing is wrong with honest criticism. Technically, criticism is only an analysis of something. The problem is that criticism usually involves an opinion of facts. Far too often opinions can either be negative or easily misunderstood as negative.

"Through hope let us find the potential that God sees in us and in others."

I was a part of a board who said they wanted to operate by a consensus of opinions. It was my first experience in such meetings, but I soon realized that a negative opinion far outweighed a positive one.

Unfortunately, most progress was thwarted because we could never get a consensus.

That particular group believed if even one person dissented to a proposal, then we could not approve the proposal. Consensus to them meant everyone had to agree. The power in saying no was enormous. It required no reason, no alternate plan, no suggestion of how to improve the proposed plan. The person just had to show a little reluctance.

In a true consensus operation, the person who is of the differing opinion from the majority should recognize that majority view. Unless the issue is of a moral or monumental consequence, the dissenters should concede for the sake of unanimity. In our group, the majority often conceded for the sake of one person with undefined, minor, negative objections. It was frustrating. It was a form of subtle, negative criticism. It was not worded harshly at all, but the effect was just as damaging to progress and morale as a bitter, critical tirade would have been.

Criticism more often comes in forms that drip with venom. I struggle with a tendency toward a critical spirit. I'm not proud of the fact that I usually know almost instinctively where the other person's jugular vein is. I have committed this problem to much prayer and thought, and yet it is still hard to hold in check at times.

Negative criticism that has no corresponding positive plan destroys projects. Such negative opinions don't build anything; they can only stop or frustrate progress. Charles Brower said, "A new idea is delicate. It can be killed by a sneer or a yawn; it can be stabbed to death by a quip and worried to death by a frown of the right man's brow."

I once was involved in a project that was held up for a couple of years. Five different committees had to be consulted and their approval gained. The project passed by those committees three or four times, each time without any dissension. However, some powerful individuals outside of our organization also had to at least look favorably on the project. Initially we received their favor, but two years of valuable time and a financial loss due to increased costs were the result of a couple of people's infectious criticism, which was outside the context of the business at hand.

Such things are not new. Moses had to deal with the critical report of the spies. Their report was full of negative criticisms. The ten spies failed to believe that God's people, who were directed by God's man, were able to go where God was leading them to receive what God had promised them.

This was Abraham Lincoln's response to critics: "If I were to try to read, much less to answer, all the attacks made on me, this shop might as well be closed for any other business. I do the very best I know how—the very best I can; and I mean to keep on doing so until the end. If the end brings me out all right, then what is said against me won't matter. If the end brings me out wrong, then ten angels swearing I was right would make no difference."

Criticisms are not always nasty remarks from someone with a critical spirit. Usually they are simply negative reports, pointing out the faults or potential hazards without pointing out any positive alternatives. Hope is not negative, it is positive. We must caution ourselves against analysis that offers no option of hope. People may try to hurt us. We may not be able to do anything about that. What we can do is protect the hope inside us that no one can destroy.

Beat the assassins. Resist the attacks. It's easier than you might think. Let hope live.

Start Small, Hope Big

One of our senior staff members in Bangladesh, Suraj Bairagee, and I were standing at the site of a new project. I started off on an exhortation of how I wanted to be sure we didn't commit too much at first to this new venture until we knew what the problems were and found good ways to expand.

Suraj stopped me midstream, anticipating my thoughts. He teasingly said, "Yes, yes, I know. Start small, hope big."

He stunned me with his concise way of summing up what he knew was my mode of operation. We had started many other projects together. By this time he knew I had big things in mind, but I was seeking practical ways to get there.

For instance, some years before, a young man came to me with a desire to be involved in audiovisual ministries. I was already interested in seeing that area of ministry developed, but until then no one had shown an interest in the media ministry. Besides that, I knew we had no extra funds to launch a venture of any size. I had always heard of the tremendous costs of electronic media, so I talked with him about our limitations.

We finally decided to add this young man to the staff with the idea to "start small, hope big." We could hardly have started any smaller than we did. In the office I had an old dictating machine left by a former missionary, some odds and ends of microphones, wires, jacks, and about a hundred new and used cassette tapes. That was all we had, but it was a beginning.

Those were small steps of faith toward what started as only a possibility, a hope. The further we stepped in faith, the bigger our hopes grew. The bigger our hopes were, the bigger our faith became. One encourages the other. That small start has now grown into a studio. Although it is still small, that ministry is one of the very few reaching the masses of the fourth or fifth largest language group in the world, which numbers over 250 million people.

"The bigger our hopes were, the bigger our faith became."

Many books on the market encourage possibilities, positive thinking, and enthusiasm. Many people criticize such concepts. Relating to the spiritual side of our lives, these concepts in themselves are not enough if our concerns are only about what we can do to improve ourselves, be more productive, and become successful. However, with a firm biblical base much can be gained from such encouragement. What are the alternatives? Should we dwell on impossibilities, negative thinking, and morbid defeat?

These philosophies cannot stand alone; neither can faith, hope, or charity stand independently. I have been stressing hope but not as a cure-all. Hope is only one aspect of the whole person. So much more needs to be added to make us well-rounded in our approach to the Christian life.

We never want to get out of balance in any direction. Rarely is a person out of balance by being too positive or too optimistic. Many more people fight depression and mull over defeats. How many times have you approached someone who is obviously in a distressed state and asked what his problem is, only to have him tell you he is suffering from too much enthusiasm? Things are just going his way too much, and he doesn't know how to handle it. How many people are burned out on hope?

Some people are naïve and some take things a little too far by being overzealous, but usually their problems are comparatively easy to correct. Give them enough strong doses of life, and they usually smarten up or slow down. A great many more people suffer from the symptoms derived from the drudgery of responsibilities and the compounding of their own interests.

Many, if not all, of the hard things we face can be handled by taking the next step. Hope is built as we take each successive step. If we can take one step, maybe we can take the next. We must not fix our minds on the huge hopeless-looking problems, on the emptiness, or on the loneliness that seems to lie ahead. The possible problems of the future are too hard to handle all at once anyway. Who says we have to handle them all now? Simply take the next step. Faith is the step; hope is the possibility that encouraged it.

Have you ever climbed a mountain? I remember the first time I climbed a mountain—it looked overwhelming! I didn't realize from the distance that there was even more to it than I thought. From a distance I could see only the face of my side of the mountain. It looked like a straight walk up to the top. I thought to myself, "It's big, but how long could that distance from the bottom to the top possibly take?" As yet the dips and valleys between the base and the peak were indiscernible.

"Faith is the step; hope is the possibility that encouraged it."

The first big valley came as a shock to me. The mountain was much larger than I had anticipated. If I had known how much of it was hidden and how difficult it can be to hike in the rarefied air of higher altitudes, I might have reconsidered starting the climb at all. Often I had to stop to catch a breath, to eat, or to regain strength, but one step at a time the mountain passed behind me. Hard times are handled like mountains. You take charge of them bit by bit.

You've heard the phrase, "Inch by inch, anything's a cinch."

A lot of hope is in that statement; it's the kind I have been advocating. Progress of any kind is encouraging. The tortoise and hare victory story is repeated when we keep on going at the pace for which we have been designed without giving in to the temptation to quit.

Not even a turtle gets anywhere until he first sticks out his neck. A tenacious tortoise mentality just keeps us sticking out our neck even though it doesn't look as if we are winning any races.

Too often we start too big and quit too soon. Don't be ashamed to start with what you have even if it is small. Don't be ashamed to hope big either.

Nothing is wrong with a big hope as long as it is based in something solid. I always want big challenging hopes, but I don't want farfetched, ridiculous dreams. Hope needs to be big enough to be challenging but never too big to be out of reason. Chasing an unreasonable hope is a time bomb of despair waiting to explode. Yet little is as fulfilling as seeing a hope develop into steps of faith and then seeing them come together as first hoped. As huge of a concept as heaven and eternal life are, they are reasonable and fulfillable because God has provided the steps to receive them.

"Hope needs to be big enough to be challenging but never too big to be out of reason."

The mountain climb I took wasn't an unreasonable climb for me. It was not the kind of mountain that required climbing vertical glass-smooth rock walls. With no equipment, no experience, and no physical training, such a climb would have been unreasonable for me to attempt. My mountain was tough enough for me, but it was not unreasonable. After that simple mountain climbing experience, maybe I could take on a tougher climb.

God has a unique way of preparing us for the challenges that come our way. With the challenges also come a God-given hope of facing and conquering the apparent obstacles.

Among the challenges we faced in the work in Bangladesh was that of few churches and workers. There had not been a residential Bible school in our mission in twenty-three years. Many attempts had been made to start one—some were good attempts—but all had failed. I began to recognize the great need for Bible training, mostly by accident.

When our family first came to Bangladesh, only about a dozen churches and about that many workers were in our mission. It was embarrassingly small. The problem with having few workers is that national workers are absolutely essential in building an indigenous church.

I had no plans to get involved with a Bible school, but soon it was glaringly apparent that we needed workers. I asked Silas Nath, one of our leaders, about who we could get to work in this new ministry opportunity. To my shock, Silas said no one was available. That was when I began to realize our great need to provide Bible training. We had no one because we had trained no one. We could build nothing there without workers.

With the irritation of missed opportunities of ministry, I began to search out the possibilities of some sort of training program. I came across the next shocking revelation. Almost no training materials were available in Bangladesh.

Silas had begun searching for books to develop a training curriculum and found little. The situation was bleak. In one of the most unreached areas of the world we had few churches. We had few churches because we had few workers. We had few workers because we had done very little training, and we had done very little training, in part, because we had very few materials to use for training.

Our church growth possibility was dismal. If my calculations were correct, and if we could somehow freeze the population, which grows at the rate of three million people a year, and if our goal was to reach every person in the nation, then at the rate of growth we were maintaining, it would have taken only 2,640,000 years to reach every person in Bangladesh!

Things didn't look good.

I really needed to know that a person has to start with the little bit he has, or he will never get to the big hope that is forming inside.

We had so very little to start a Bible school with. First we worked on translating training materials. The process was painfully slow and very expensive. I would return to the States after each four-year term for a year of raising support and visiting churches only to meet pastors and missionaries who were having great successes.

I had friends who were building great churches with hundreds and even thousands in attendance. I had no glorious reports. I had only stories of how we had survived and how much need still existed. It was all true, and it was very discouraging. Few people get excited over another translated book.

Finally we started the school. We had very little money and only one full-time staff member, but we started. Starting is important. All the motivational books say it in a different way, but they all say the same thing: You have to begin.

We set our criteria for the kind of students we wanted in the school. We didn't set the standard too high, but we had a standard. We required only four things of students who wanted to come. We wanted students who confessed a salvation experience, who were full of the Holy Spirit, and who felt that God had called them into full-time ministry. Besides that, we wanted the highest level students available, so we wanted those who had at least passed their HSC exams, which is equivalent to a high school diploma.

Not a single application came. Zilch. Zip. Zero.

We finally realized our standard was maybe a little too high for the students available. We decided that for the first year it might be all right to drop our educational standard a little bit.

No takers. Zilch. Zip. Zero.

Finally we reached the point that we accepted students if they said they were born-again and if they could read! Some of them were not telling the truth! Three students couldn't read well enough to be in school.

I remember the awful feeling I had as I looked at the first group of village boys who could barely sign their names. We had worked for years getting that far—and this was all we had!

The Lord spoke to Zechariah saying, "Who despises the day of small things?" (Zechariah 4:10). I was very near to being one of those who despises small things. This feeble beginning was one of those small things not to be despised: Those young men ended up going out to pastor in some of the toughest, loneliest spots on earth.

Each year they were joined by another handful of uneducated, unqualified, young men. In a little over six years over a hundred churches and outstations had developed, and the school was enrolling more and more students each year.

Many people get stuck at the starting line trying to decide whether or not to get in the race. Even a tortoise with a destination has to at least start.

Hoping big is not hard. Starting small isn't hard either if you can get past the feeling that what you have or what you are is too small. Beginning is indeed a major part of the battle, but holding on until the end is the other major part of it. The continuous building of one small thing after another gets tedious, especially if you look, feel, and act like a tortoise.

A couple of companion phrases of warning similar to the "inch by inch" maxim are "yard by yard, anything's hard" and "mile by mile, anything's a trial." Be careful not to develop a disdain for the simple, the ordinary, the small.

Marathon racers don't quit in the first mile nor do they quit in the last mile. They usually quit in one of those middle miles when neither the starting line nor the finish line is in sight. The hurting legs and lungs make their call for the runner to quit. The hope to conquer the big challenge is not the next mile; it's the next step.

CHAPTER ELEVEN

Beyond Fantasyland

Imagination is a God-given gift that helps us in our creative abilities when properly used. Although it may encourage a hopeful attitude and allow us to visualize some of our hopes, imagination in itself falls short of the kind of hope we need. Hope says something is possible even when it looks impossible; imagination paints the picture.

Mental picture painting is what imagination does best. The kind of hope we need is available even on rainy days when we have a cold, the baby is crying, and our creative, imaginative minds are seeing ugly pictures rather than bright ones. Such imagination can lead us away from hope rather than to it. Imagination tends to swing with moods, whereas hope is rock solid.

Imagination can also create pictures in the mind that have little to do with reality. We can create images that can never be brought into actual existence. Some of the pictures of Hindu gods and goddesses, such as Ganesh with the elephant head, Durga with the many arms, or Kali with the many heads of her husband and enemies hanging from her neck and with the ever-present blood, emphasize how dangerous imagination can be when one believes the image is a reality.

If we believe that all we imagine is hope and can be brought to existence by faith, we might be in danger of a very subtle deception. Although imagination can be a tremendous mental asset, if it is unchecked, it can go beyond God-given spiritual reality. We must not allow ourselves to be deceived into believing that hope and imagination are the same, even though they can both be tremendously used by God. We need to learn to differentiate between the two.

The kind of hope that will last through the hard times is based in God. Imagination in itself, no matter how hopeful it seems, is based in us. When imagination and hope meet, imagination needs to always be subordinate to a God-given hope. Imagination must also undergo biblical and spiritual checks to be sure it remains in line with purposes of God.

> **"We must not allow ourselves to be deceived into believing that hope and imagination are the same, even though they can both be tremendously used by God."**

Some people express big imaginative hopes, thinking their hope is faith. One person shared his dream of a multimillion dollar project dedicated to Jesus and world missions. Almost in the next breath he asked me to remember him in prayer for his small struggling business. Something just didn't fit together. I don't want to belittle his hope in any way because God has asked people to do some unusual things in the past. I don't want to share bleacher seats with the mockers.

I must remember arks, Red Sea crossings, and activities of the Old Testament prophets. Some of the things the prophets of God did are almost too weird for words, yet they were of God. We need to learn to differentiate between "pie in the sky" imaginative hope and a solid biblical hope that must include the outstanding miraculous hand of God.

Discernment must also be made between the miraculous and the fantastic. My hope includes the miracles of God but not all of the fantastic of this world. We must look at the source. Real miracles come from God; the fantastic may or may not. We need to discern what the source is.

The outgrowth of imagination can be either directed toward a real hope or an unreal fantasy. I would like to make a few observations about extremes of the fantastic.

A friend who had spent the first thirty-some years of his life in poverty in the third world made a first-time visit to the United States. Discussing his experiences in the States, I asked him if he had visited Disneyland. He replied, "Of course! Your whole country is Disneyland!" I had to agree. We Americans like the fantastic. Our movies and television are heavy into the fantastic. Many Americans deal with an enormous amount of fantasy every day through television and other media. For some, the flood of fantasy drowns out reality. Many people are actually more comfortable with the imaginative than with the real.

We have a tremendous power to focus on the electronic images flashing on the television. The mind has a difficult time denying that what it sees is real. We laugh and cry and easily become emotionally involved because we are touched through the open gates of our imagination. Standards of style, behavior, and even morality are influenced as we get involved in the fantasy.

Without the fantastic, it is nearly impossible to get the attention of many people. Our malls and stores are in constant decorative changes and in so many ways seem to come straight out of Fantasyland.

In America everything is super, huge, special, great, terrific, stupendous, fantastic, magical, spectacular, enormous, colossal, gigantic, tremendous, whopping, superhuman, sensational. It has to be in order to sell or to grab the human imagination. Miraculous fits into the list of superlatives without much notice. Yet it is supposed to be different.

The story is told of one little boy who went to Sunday school for the first time. At home his mother asked him what Bible story he had learned. He replied, "Moses crossing the Red Sea." His mother wanted to hear all about it.

The little boy began, "Well, you see, there was this guy Moses and a bunch of people with him being chased out of Egypt by Pharaoh's army. Pharaoh was coming on hard with his tanks and assault helicopters, and Moses was trapped at the Red Sea. Then Moses radioed the Air Force to lay a smoke screen in front of Pharaoh while the Army Corps of Engineers constructed a pontoon bridge for Moses to cross the Red Sea.

"Then the Navy Seals mined the bridge, and they waited for Pharaoh's army to get on the bridge. When the army was on the bridge, Moses had the Navy Seals blow it up. At the same time, the artillery was firing, and missiles were shooting the helicopters out of the sky. Moses totally wiped them out!"

Astonished, his mother asked, "Is that really the way your teacher told you the story?" To which he replied, "No, but you wouldn't have believed it the way she told it!"

We are living in a world where, for many, miracles seem to be unbelievable. Because they are often so unbelievable to modern man, the miracles of the Bible are explained away in modern terms and reasoning. Yet that same modern man may choose to believe some amazing things because of his exposure to the fantastic world of movie wizardry.

The miraculous hand of God sometimes seems mild compared with the movies. We live in a society that has grown to expect the fantastic. Movie makers keep creating some of the most amazing visual fantasies. Commercials capture the attention and hold it for thirty seconds. In that brief time they inform and create a desire for the product and a whole attitude about the kind of person who uses their product.

"We have fed an appetite for the spectacular to the place where many often prefer the fantastic creations of man to the miracles of God."

We have no lack of imagination in America. What many do lack is an appreciation for spiritual reality. We have fed an appetite for the spectacular to the point where many often prefer the fantastic creations of man to the miracles of God. They are often more eye-catching than miracles. In fact, the miracles of God and the hope created by them are often being explained in terms of the fantastic creative genius of modern man through science and technology.

Our society is rapidly turning toward a materialistic humanism, and yet has a strange love for the superhuman and supernatural. Oddly many people reject the possibility of an actual immanent and transcendent God while such a hunger for the supernatural is expressed.

The God of the Bible is both immanent and transcendent. He is ever with us. He is immanent and touches the material and physical needs of man. Yet He is a God who is so much greater and beyond us in His transcendence. He is fantastically beyond mere fantasy.

We need God in both His immanence and His transcendence. We need Him in the practical, understandable strength of the daily routine of life, and at the same time we need God who is greater than life—supernaturally able to do that which is beyond understanding.

How is it that there is such a rejection of this immanence and transcendence of God in the secular world when there is such an increasing interest in the meta-physical and the material?

Even though in practical terms materialism is widely taught and accepted in our culture, it is not a pure philosophical materialism. Materialism is only that which is observable and provable. Only physical matter is believed by many to be ultimately real. True materialism, however, would not accept those things that are "super." Instead, in our American materialism there is, in practical terms, a replacement for the transcendent. It is the love for the fantastic that captures the imagination. In America we have *super* everything.

If we have grown accustomed to such a diet of fantasy and superlatives, how much of that mind-set has entered our view of spiritual reality? In a mind-set of the fantastic, what does a person believe an act of faith is? What are our hopes? Have we based our expectations on imaginations or biblical hope? Are we looking for man or for God to save us?

In such an atmosphere does our spouse need to be a superspouse to be acceptable? Are we disappointed if our children aren't superachievers? Must our pastor be bigger than life in his abilities and wisdom?

If we eat fantastic flakes, use supersexy cologne, brush with toothpaste that gives ultrabrilliance because of its extraspecial secret ingredient, drive a sporty (or elegant) car while listening to "now" music on a state of the art sound system and talking on our cellular phone that interfaces with our microcompact computer (with ever-increasing megabytes), can we become superhuman enough to fit into this world and be satisfied? No.

And where does God fit into all of this? Hope in Him cuts right through all the emptiness of the fantastic world of humanistic imagination and puts us in contact with the eternally real. In hope we begin to see that something much more fulfilling exists. Life in Jesus is not eternally dull. It is far beyond our vain attempts to create moods and atmosphere. It is life-conscious more than life-style-conscious.

As I have mentioned, one outgrowth of imagination is fantasy. Maybe I have warned about the dangerous side so strongly that you think I'm against imaginative creativity. I'm not. Both the fantastic and the imaginative can be used creatively for the good. They are not intrinsically wrong. The misuse of these, knowingly or otherwise, concerns me. The seductive trends that unknowingly dictate our thinking trouble me. The distortions of imagination are wrong.

Many of us aren't imaginative enough with our presentation of the gospel to the world. I have one friend who uses both the imaginative and the fantastic to capture the attention of the lost who wouldn't otherwise cross the doorstep of any church to hear the gospel. He says he would stand on this head stacking BBs while playing his trombone if it would create interest in someone long enough for them to stop and listen to the message of salvation that he is so skilled in presenting. The difference is that he directs the fantastic toward the things of God rather than away from Him. He simply realizes that the kind of world we live in makes it difficult to get the needed attention to deliver any idea.

In writing this I have focused on extremes. We live in a sensual world. Most people want to know what truth is. They also seem to have a great need to feel something extraspecial. Too many times the need for the extraspecial feeling is realized at the expense of truth. It doesn't have to be.

We can sense the presence of God. We can feel His closeness. When we do, we realize He is so much greater than all the inventive pizzazz of this world.

If you have not had a close experiential encounter with the Lord, I encourage you to seek that personal relationship with the eternal God of truth. If you know Him "in spirit and in truth," you will readily agree there is no thrill or specialness in this world that compares to those special spiritual encounters we have with God. In an instant of such spiritual times when He reveals himself as our God, we know He is enough to thrill and fulfill us for eternity. Hope in Jesus is beyond our greatest imagination. He is utterly and superbly fantastic.

CHAPTER TWELVE

The Beginning

Flying between the Orient and the United States can play havoc on your schedule if you don't carefully consider the crossing of the international date line. I was on a flight from Bangkok with the first United States stop in Los Angeles when I noticed on my arrival schedule that I was to arrive in Los Angeles ten minutes after I began the trip! The next week on my return flight, although I was taking the same route in reverse with about the same flying time, I was to arrive in Bangkok two days after I had started. On that return flight going west across the date line, it hit me that someplace over the Pacific I flew right into tomorrow!

Hope is futuristic. It takes us into tomorrow while our watches are still set for the present.

Think about it. Hope is never an activity of the "present." The only way to bring hope into the present is through faith. Hope is always looking forward to the possibilities, but in hope they remain only possibilities. We can hope there is a God just as a child can hope there is a Santa Claus, but hoping doesn't bring the reality into our lives. Faith recognizes the substance in hope and acts upon it. We accept the reality of the future in our hope and in faith commit ourselves now, not tomorrow, nor yesterday. The past contains no hope, only memories. Hope is a foundational part of all of our tomorrows.

Faith is most often seen as a New Testament reality. In the New International Version of the Bible, *faith* is mentioned 16 times in the Old

Testament. In the New Testament the word occurs 254 times. *Hope* is found in both the Old Testament and New Testament almost equally. The central figure of the Bible is Jesus. The Old Testament could only point toward the coming Messiah in hope that He would come soon. The New Testament, along with hope, has a different, dynamic faith.

"Faith recognizes the substance in hope and acts upon it."

Judson Cornwall points out "that hope is never attributed to Jesus, nor did the word ever cross His lips except for the occasion, when He referred to 'your hope.' For Him the realities of the next world and of the future were so completely familiar that He did not need hope."

We do not see heavenly realities as clearly as Jesus did. We often still need hope to lead us to the immediacy of faith. As important as it is to begin with a strong hope, it is temporary for us. However, its temporary nature doesn't minimize the importance of hope. We simply need to realize hope is temporary until we begin to act or accept the thing hoped for in faith. Hope sees tomorrow; faith acts as though it is today.

As the Old Testament looked toward the coming of the Messiah, the New Testament looks toward His Second Coming. Titus 2:13 calls that expectancy the "blessed hope." Notice that it is not called our "blessed faith." There is an understanding there of the human element that is not sure how to deal with the unknown areas of death. We are not sure experientially what the end means for us personally. We can be biblically sure and resolute in our understanding and yet still not be ready to grab faith for death or even the Second Coming so easily. Hope sustains us.

I can't say I always live with a keen anticipation of Christ's coming. I have plans. I have a fairly clear idea of what I will be doing per hour for the next few months. I have twenty years of mortgage payments and a one-year fixed deposit. My insurance policy matures in less than twenty-five years. I currently live in five-year intervals made up of four years overseas and one year in the United States. I have a two-year calendar, a five-year program of church growth for the work we are involved in, and speaking engagements booked two years from now. Our denomination has a Decade of Harvest for the 90s, with a set of goals for each year. Yes, I believe Jesus is coming, but if it isn't now, I have contingency plans. I have plans to survive until Jesus comes, whenever that might be!

In all practicality, because of my plans, I will probably be taken off guard just as much as the next person when Jesus comes in the twinkling of an eye. Spiritually, in the sight of God, I am ready for His return. My salvation is sure. However, my feelings are not always so sure nor is my expectancy level high.

Have you ever had one of those times of Rapture alarm when you wake up from a nap or come in from some secluded location and no one is there? Things around the neighborhood are unusually quiet. Everything is in place as though people should be there, but they aren't. You call one of the most holy of saints, and no one answers. After an inordinate amount of time, as you are looking through your library for end-time prophecy books, someone finally comes. After checking his forehead and the back of his hand for telltale marks, you begin to relax. You realize you haven't been left behind because of some secret sin or doctrinal error after all.

Such times are startling, but rare. Much of the time we get caught up in survival or in trying vainly to repair a piece of this broken world. We forget our hope is not of this world.

Our hope is Jesus. He is the hidden mystery of the ages of Colossians 1. He is "Christ in you, the hope of glory" (Colossians 1:27). In Hebrews He is the one who is the same "yesterday and today and forever" (13:8). I have assurance in Him because in all of my yesterdays He has proven to be reliable. I have faith in Him because He is helping me today. Therefore why should I have any doubt about my forever future relationship with the Lord?

In the gallery in the Vatican in Rome are some of the Christian inscriptions taken from the catacombs. On the other side of the gallery are inscriptions that were written on the Roman temples. One inscription from the Roman temples was the dismal words, "Farewell,

farewell, and forever farewell." But an inscription from the catacombs said these words, "He who dies in Christ dies in peace and hope." Jesus told us He would go and prepare a place for us. We also know He is coming again, and the saints will meet Him in the clouds. What is our hope in the end of history? I used to think it was pearly gates, streets of gold, and mansions. That's what many songs and imaginative evangelists had taught me. Those things weren't that much of an incentive to me as a young man. Where is the excitement in a great house in a perfect neighborhood? Frankly, most harp music bores me.

"Hope is a foundational part of all of our tomorrows."

What are we offering to a lost world as an everlasting hope? Is it just the best of two choices, or something overwhelmingly worthy of our blessed hope?

The descriptions of heaven contain some limitations. God was inspiring writers to describe the indescribable. How do you describe that which is beyond words when all you have available to use are words?

Earthbound biblical writers were limited to earthly figurative language in trying to describe the vision or revelation God had given them of heavenly things. Can you imagine the frustration?

I tried once to describe what an American shopping mall is to a man in a village in Bangladesh. How do you describe things like express check-out lanes, cash registers, price scanners, bar codes, gumball machines, Muzak, blue-light specials, and shopping carts to people whose idea of a shop is limited to thirty or forty items in a four-by five- by eight-foot bamboo shack where the owner, wearing a skirt, shirt, and sandals, sits on a wood plank all day because the ceiling is too low to stand? Then try to tell the villager that this mere "shop" you are describing is bigger, nicer, and cleaner than any building he could see in his own land. Can you imagine the difficulty?

Have you ever tried to describe the taste of a new food or the scent of a new cologne? It isn't easy to describe the indescribable. You can see the difficulty for those who wrote about the eternal realm. What words do you use to describe heaven? What is it like? If it is so totally unlike anything else ever seen or experienced, how does a person convey with mere words its wonder? Whatever it is like, it must be spectacular because the most precious materials known to us were quickly depleted on an explanation of gates and streets alone!

As wonderful as the accommodations and furnishings of heaven must be, our material description doesn't easily excite a middle or higher income American in the suburbs. We are so blessed that heavenly material splendor is not a highly motivating attraction. What hope then is great enough for those who are trapped in the poverty of Somalia and for both those who, by no choice or merit of their own, were born into wealth?

The majesty of God himself as Father, Holy Spirit, and especially Jesus the Son will so outshine the place itself that the jeweled crowns of the twenty-four elders will be cast down at the feet of Him who sits on the throne. Before Him crowns are of no value. Jesus, in His glory in the Godhead, will be the thrill of heaven for the redeemed. Worshiping Him will be a joyous activity beyond any we have ever known.

Wouldn't the God who created the heavens and the earth and provides the possibilities for all the simple joys we know here on earth provide even greater things in a greater place? Let us not limit the creativity of the Creator in our inability to picture what heaven and its agenda will be.

Heaven: streets of gold, harps, angels with blond hair and large wings, and mansions—Maybe the stereotype of heaven is boring, but that's not God's fault. We have simply failed to let our hope of heaven be great enough. Imagine heaven as eternally existing as you are able to; picture it as spectacularly beautiful as possible; read the passages of promise again; stretch your thinking as far as you are able; add as much joy as you can possibly conceive; then multiply it all by the largest number ever calculated. My guess is you're not even close to the wonders of eternity with Jesus. In heavenly things let us not limit hope!

I worked for nearly ten years with Mark and Gladys Bliss. They were missions veterans of many years who worked in African countries and Iran before joining the work in Bangladesh. Better people can't be found.

In 1970, Mark and Gladys, their two teenage daughters and their son were traveling at night in Iran in their car. With them were an Iranian pastor and his child. A truck had stopped over the crest of a hill in their lane. Their car hit the truck, killing the three Bliss children, the child of the Iranian pastor, and badly hurting Gladys.

Mark had to deal with the trauma of the deaths and hospitalization of some of the dearest people in his life. He also had the struggle of dealing with the authorities who wanted to jail him for the accident because citizens had died.

When Mark returned home for the first time after the accident, Gladys was still in the hospital with a badly damaged leg. Mark went into the empty rooms of each of his children. Toys, books, clothes, and other belongings were in the same place they had been before the family had begun their journey. The Bible of the Bliss' daughter Debbie was open on the bed where she had left it after having her own personal devotions before the trip.

Mark quietly walked through the house, sat down at the organ, and began to sing "It Is Well with My Soul."

Some years later the Blisses came to work in Bangladesh. At that time Ron Peck was the area representative for Southern Asia. The work in Bangladesh was within his area of responsibility, so he traveled in and out of the country frequently. On one of those visits he had been loaned the Bible that had belonged to Debbie Bliss. On his way to his meeting he thumbed through her Bible and noticed the many places where Debbie had underlined precious passages of Scripture for herself. Then Ron noticed the last page where Revelation 22:20 says, "He who testifies to these things says, 'Yes, I am coming soon.' Amen. Come, Lord Jesus. The grace of the Lord Jesus be with God's people. Amen." In Debbie's King James Version of the Bible the publishers had printed, "The End." Debbie had taken an ink pen and marked through those two words of finality to the point that the pen had begun to cut through the paper. Then she had written below it, "The Beginning."

"Where, O death, is your victory? Where, O death, is your sting?" (1 Corinthians 15:55). The Lord himself will come down from heaven, with a loud command, with the voice of the archangel and with the trumpet call of God, and the dead in Christ will rise first. After that, we who are still alive and are left will be caught up together with them in the clouds to meet the Lord in the air. And so we will be with the Lord forever" (1 Thessalonians 4:16-17).

Death is in many ways mysterious to us. Fear of it has often caused an undue dread. The promises of the Bible are clear enough; death is the fulfillment of those promises we aren't too sure of. What is it *really* like to die? Our apprehension about death often kills our hope.

Cancer for the Christian is not terminal; it is temporary. We are not facing the end; we are expectantly anticipating the beginning—our blessed hope. Remember, our hope is not heaven; our hope is Jesus.

Many years ago I was for a short time the assistant pastor in a church in Panama City, Florida. I was impatiently awaiting the day I could go overseas as a missionary. Not long after going to the church, we received the news of a tragic death of a young missionary named Aubrey Lamp.

The church we were in was Aubrey's home church, yet I never had had the opportunity to meet him. My wife and I attended the funeral, mostly out of respect for the family we did know. With my interest in missions, I was especially sensitive to the apparent loss to the work of God in a faraway land. I expected the service to have a more somber tone than usual because a servant of God had been taken tragically in the beginning of a ministry that had been his lifelong dream.

To my surprise, the funeral of Aubrey Lamp was the most jubilant funeral service I had ever attended. The songs were uplifting, and the mood of the service was triumphant. I began to view the death of a Christian in a new way. This was not a loss; it was a transition. It was a celebration of Aubrey's entrance into what he had hoped for.

Several years later, the pastor of my own home church, H. W. Barnett, went to be with the Lord. His ministry of over forty years had helped prepare over fifty of us from that church for full-time ministry. His son,

Tommy Barnett, preached the service. It was not a time of wailing and mourning the loss of this great servant of God; instead, it was a time of recalling the triumphant ministry of a man who had been faithful and had done a great work for God.

The experiences of these funerals has helped me face my own future death. I want to come to the end stronger in the Lord and more sure of following Him than when I started. I want no regrets as I cross the finish line. I want to be able to say I gave my best to Jesus. My desire is that those who remain will recognize it too.

This may seem morbid, but I have already told people what I want at my funeral! I want everyone who attends to sing my favorite Christian song, "The Old Rugged Cross." Then I want someone who really knows how to take an offering to collect the biggest offering for missions they possibly can. After that I want the most capable evangelistic preacher they can find to preach as triumphant a message as possible about Jesus and our blessed hope. Then I want them to give as persuasive an altar call as possible and invite people to trust in the Lord as Savior. I want people to know that death for the believer is not an end in hopelessness. It is the beginning, the beginning of more than we have ever hoped for in Jesus!

CHAPTER THIRTEEN

Don't Give Up Hope

Who can take away our hope?

My personal well-being, my emotional and mental health, is very dependent on where I have placed my hope. If my hope can be destroyed, then I can be destroyed. If my hope can't be destroyed, then there is no fear of an ultimate failure. If hope is that important, then I want the strongest possible hope. I need to be so sure of my hope that no disaster, no loss, no person, and no devil in hell can take it away.

The Book of Hebrews has a key to the kind of hope that is so strong no one can take it away from us except for one person. We must be careful of that one person.

Look at the passage in Hebrews 6:19-20: "We have this hope as an anchor for the soul, firm and secure. It enters the inner sanctuary behind the curtain, where Jesus, who went before us, has entered on our behalf. He has become a high priest forever, in the order of Melchizedek."

The insecurity of being in a boat that is tossing in a boisterous sea of potentially devastating waves, which could sink the boat or drive it into the rocks, is very descriptive of life's hazards. The anchor holds the boat and prevents the destruction. Hope is the anchor for the soul.

In this passage is a sudden shift of pictures. The first picture is of the anchor that can hold in storms. Suddenly the picture goes from an earthly, raging sea to a picture of the heavenly Holy of Holies.

That sudden shift comes where the sentence starts with the word *it.* We understand clearly that the anchor of the soul is talking about our hope, but what is this "it"? Look at that "it" again. Notice that "it" enters the "inner sanctuary behind the curtain." The place is clear enough. The picture is a place inside the heavenly Holy of Holies.

We then are told that Jesus has entered before us and on our behalf because He is our High Priest, but He is not the same kind of high priest as under the Levitical system. He is a different kind. He is like Melchizedek.

"I need to be sure of my hope that no disaster, no loss, no person, and no devil in hell can take it away."

Melchizedek is later described in Hebrews as being a priest of a different order and type of priesthood. The author argues rightly, because Abraham gave tithes to Melchizedek. His order of priesthood was greater than that of the later Levitical system that came through Abraham.

Hebrews describes Jesus as a priest after this order going into the Holy of Holies, even though Melchizedek could never have gone into a Holy of Holies on this earth. The system had not yet been instated. Yet because of the higher order, Jesus has access to that most Holy Place.

Notice then that not only does Jesus have access, He is also a forerunner. In the tabernacle and in the temple where the earthly Holy of Holies was, only the high priest had access. Yet in this picture in the heavenlies, others evidently have access; they are the redeemed. A forerunner must indicate that others are following. However, they cannot go in without a high priest, without a pure sacrifice, nor without an advocate having first pled their case.

Still what is this "it"? This "it" does not appear to be referring to Jesus who is mentioned just afterward. In the line of thought that has proceeded, the "it" seems to be clearly talking about hope. If so, what is the message that we are to understand?

I believe the strong message that the Lord wants us to know is that God makes promises to His people that will be kept. These are promises of substance because they come from God himself. He has sealed them with an oath and has sworn by the most awesome of assurances we could possibly have: His very existence. God has sworn by the integrity of His own name that the promises are sure.

We are also reminded that His unchangeable. When He says it, it is. When he promises it, it will be. We further know God does not lie. Therefore, these promises are more solid than the earth itself because they come from the Creator of the earth. So when we receive a promise from God, hope is created in our hearts. It is a strong hope that is backed up by God himself.

Let's get back to the "it" again. "It" is the hope that comes from knowing what God promised; "it enters the inner sanctuary." Again, this is out of the ordinary because the only things that are to enter into the Holy of Holies are the high priest in his sanctified garments and the sacrifice of blood.

Allow me to create a scenario of how this event could take place. Remember, the scene is in the heavenlies. Entering into the holiest place of all is Jesus, our forerunner and High Priest of the higher order. He is getting ready to go where no one has gone and open the way for us, the redeemed, to follow.

As Jesus enters, God the Father, the judge of all righteousness, is watching and judging to see if He has met the standard of purity required for entry. Jesus' garments are spotless, and He himself is holy. The Father will accept only the blood of a pure sacrifice. The sacrifice that Jesus has is more pure than any of the sacrifices before. It is the blood of the spotless Lamb of God—Jesus' own blood. Then the Father notices something else. With Jesus is that "it" we've been talking about. I can imagine the conversation.

Knowing that nothing else but that which has been fore-ordained should enter the Holy of Holies, the Father has the responsibility to ask, "What is it that you have with you?"

"It is hope," replies Jesus.

The Father further questions, "Whose hope is this?"

"This is the hope of Larry Smith and that of millions of others," answers Jesus.

"How is it that you bring it into this most Holy Place?" the Father asks.

Jesus, who is also a part of the Godhead, replies, "Because they have put their hope in us."

"Does it pass all the qualifications of purity for us to accept this hope?" questions the Father.

Jesus, who is also our advocate and knows heavenly procedure, says, "Yes, most assuredly we should honor this hope. I have died for this hope and have the stripes on my back for this hope. Besides that, we don't lie or change. We have made promises concerning this hope."

The Father goes further, "But nothing enters here except that which has been purified by blood."

Jesus, the Lamb of God, quickly answers, "My blood has been given for this hope, because in this hope is all of our purposes for humanity who has been created in our image. They have trusted us with this hope."

"Where did they get this hope?" asks God the Father.

"I have examined this hope and have seen that this is not a hope they created on their own. It has come from us. We gave it to them, didn't we?" says the Son.

Realizing that all the requirements have been met, the Father consults with the Son on one last point of responsibility—the part of the commitment of the Godhead to this hope. "Is there anything that would keep us from our responsibility of honoring this hope of Larry Smith and the millions of others?" the Father inquires.

The Son answers, "There is no way for us not to honor this hope. It has been given by us, sanctified by my blood, and entrusted to us knowing that we do not change or lie. There is no way now for us not to honor this hope nor would we want to. There is absolutely no way not to honor this great hope," Jesus hesitates for a moment, "except for one."

The Father asks the Son, "What is that one way which would keep us from such a responsibility of fulfilling this hope bearing our name and approval?"